CONVERSATIONS WITH MONTGOMERY

Conversations
with
Montgomery

ANTONY BRETT-JAMES

WILLIAM KIMBER · LONDON

First published in 1984 by
WILLIAM KIMBER & CO. LIMITED
100 Jermyn Street, London, SW1Y 6EE

© Estate of Antony Brett-James, 1984
ISBN 0-7183-0531-0

Filmset by Cheney & Sons Limited, Banbury
and printed and bound in Great Britain by
Biddles Limited, Guildford and King's Lynn

Contents

List of Illustrations

Acknowledgements

The author and publishers would like to express their gratitude to the Viscount Montgomery of Alamein, CBE, for this kind permission to quote from his father's writings.

I

It all began with Field-Marshal Lord Alanbrooke. In July 1963 I had been working for eighteen months as a lecturer in Military History at the Royal Military Academy Sandhurst. I was invited by the BBC to put together and present an appreciation of Alanbrooke as a professional soldier and as Britain's wartime Chief of the Imperial General Staff. I had never done anything like this before. Nor had I served in the Royal Artillery — Alanbrooke had been Master Gunner. I had not served under his command, still less had I met the great man. It is true that I had watched him receive life membership of the Union Society at Cambridge soon after the war, and had by chance stood beside the stooping figure dressed in khaki when we used the urinal after the ceremony was over. And I had once heard him lecture about an ornithological expedition to southern Spain. But these were very tenuous links with a formidable soldier who had died only three weeks before, within reach of his eightieth birthday.

The next five months proved to be a wonderfully interesting journey of discovery, first among the diaries which had been edited for publication by Arthur Bryant and which I read again with infinitely greater care, and then among a handful of the men and women who had known Alanbrooke at various stages of his distinguished life. Selection of the team of contributors who would describe the man, his methods of work, his relations with colleagues, his ways of finding relaxation from the immense burdens of high office, and his part in the winning of the Second World War – all this was a challenge.

One of the obvious contributors was Field-Marshal Montgomery, and as he and two others lived near Sandhurst, I suggested to the producer, Neil Crichton-Miller, that we should record them at home rather than in a studio. So on Friday, 18th October, after lunch in the officers' mess, we drove first to see Montgomery at his converted mill house in Isington, a hamlet just below the Farnham-Alton road near Bentley.

What a very different sort of field-marshal from Alanbrooke: less practical, much narrower in his skills and interests, a man with almost no relaxations, certainly of the Alanbrooke style. For instance, it was hard to picture Montgomery fishing, or scything long grass, or browsing in specialist bookshops, or watching birds, still less building imaginary houses with his driver during long car journeys. But these were early days, and I for one had neither met, nor even set eyes on, the famous 'Monty', even though I had spent six weeks under his command in the Alamein Line during August and September 1942.

The gates of Isington Mill were open, and as I drove in I spotted the Field-Marshal's small trim figure at the far end of the garden. He was talking to the gardener, but heard the car and began walking towards us across the lawn.

He led us into a long hangar on the left of the drive, and then into his principal wartime caravan. Montgomery remarked: 'I always do these things in here', almost as if such recordings happened once a week. While the BBC engineer fixed up his machine on a small table, the Field-Marshal opened a drawer and took out two sheets of plain foolscap paper on which he had written in pencil what he proposed to say. The first piece dealt with Brooke as a corps commander in France during the 1940 campaign, when Lord Gort led the British Expeditionary Force. Montgomery started on a contentious note:

> Alanbrooke had no confidence in Gort. He was far superior to Gort in brain power, military ability, and character. When the crisis burst on the French and British armies on the 10 May 1940, Gort did his best to make up for past unrealism. He had in Alanbrooke a Corps Commander who was steady as a rock in adversity.

This part I cut from the eventual programme. Montgomery went on:

> I saw a great deal of him during the withdrawal from the British front on the River Dyle back to the Dunkirk bridgehead; he commanded in what I consider is the right way to command – he visited his Divisional Commanders, of whom I was one*, at the right moments, gave his orders so clearly that they could not possibly be misunderstood, and never gave any sign of his inner disquiet.
>
> I have no hesitation in saying that if it had not been for Alanbrooke, we would never have got the bulk of the trained officers and men of the B.E.F. safely back to England – and if we had not done *that* we would never

*Montgomery commanded the 3rd Division, part of Brooke's II Corps.

have been able to build up military strength in the country as quickly as we did.

That was what he had written. However I had been reading more about Alanbrooke since I had first been in touch with Montgomery, so asked whether he would say something about the circumstances in which Alanbrooke was ordered back to England:

'In your memoirs, sir, you wrote that he was very upset; and General Horrocks says that he appeared to be weeping, and you were patting him on the back.'

'You didn't ask for that in your letter,' said the Field-Marshal with a challenging but not unfriendly look. He then agreed to add a few sentences, straight 'off the cuff' without notes.

'Of course Alanbrooke had to be sent back to England before the final evacuation. He didn't want to go and he was very, very upset about it and came to see me and told me I was to take over command of his corps. And he completely broke down and really burst into tears at having to leave his command. But I told him that if anybody must be saved from this racket, and it didn't look as if anybody *would* be saved, at least *he* must be, because he was the *one* person who could take command of the British Army next time we went overseas.'

Crichton-Miller and I thanked him warmly for that extra vignette, and then made ready to record his second piece, which was an assessment of Alanbrooke's relations as Chief of the Imperial General Staff with his commanders in the field.

This was his pencilled script:

Alanbrooke became C.I.G.S. at the end of 1941 and at once became immersed in tremendous problems. These were connected with the capture of our territories in the Far East by the Japanese, the disasters of the first Burma campaign, the setback in the Western Desert — everywhere we were being thrown back on the defensive.

It was essential under these conditions that Alanbrooke should establish his authority over army commanders as professional head of the British Army. He did this in no uncertain way by his force of character, his great knowledge of the conduct of war, and by his warm-hearted support in times of adversity. In those days before the Americans came fully into action, we British worked on the committee system of management in the various theatres — a trinity of the three Service chiefs, in which the soldier was generally the chairman of the committee.

Later, Supreme Commanders were adopted and then Alanbrooke had to act more warily. For instance, I myself was serving directly under Eisenhower. But I always kept in the closest touch with Alanbrooke, and his advice was the best I knew — far better than that of my Supreme Commander.

I deleted this controversial last sentence from the broadcast programme. I had been particularly intrigued by a photograph in his *Memoirs* of Churchill, Alanbrooke and Montgomery lunching on the east bank of the Rhine, on 26th March 1945. Would the Field-Marshal, I asked, be prepared to say a little about visits by Churchill?

'Certainly,' he replied briskly:

'The Prime Minister used to visit the armies in the field a great deal, and Alanbrooke always came with him. I think you can say this about Winston Churchill, that he was a person who must always dominate, but when he was in the zone of the army with me, he admitted that he must do as I told him, because I was the Commander-in-chief. We had many picnics together, he and I and Alanbrooke; and there's a very famous one when we all three sat down at a little table on the banks of the Rhine and had lunch together, and talked about how we should handle the future.'

Then, as an afterthought, he said he could tell us a story about that photograph – 'But you mustn't broadcast it. It's not for the programme.' He chuckled.

'After lunch Winston asked me: "Is that the River Rhine, Monty?" "Yes, sir." "Good! Well I'm going to pee in it." He stood up and walked to the bank and pee-ed in the Rhine.' Montgomery gave us quite a good imitation of Churchill's voice.

When the BBC engineer had packed up his recording equipment, Montgomery accompanied us to the car, but he made no move to show us the other two caravans in the hangar or the house itself. We drove off to record Alanbrooke's driver, Sergeant Percy Parker, who proved to have the most illuminating things to say of anyone in the programme.

I never expected to meet the Field-Marshal again. I was wrong.

II

My real association with Montgomery began a year later when the Library at Sandhurst organised an exhibition to mark, a trifle late, the twentieth anniversary of D-Day and the battle for Normandy. It was to run from 29th November 1964 until the end of term on 18th December. I became very involved in helping to mount the exhibition, and one day I suggested to the Reader in Military History, Brigadier Peter Young, that Monty might be willing to lend us one or two personal relics of that summer of 1944. It would be worth approaching him, especially as he lived so near.

Peter liked my suggestion and asked me to draft a letter to Monty which he could sign. I did so. After an opening sentence the letter ran:

We have already arranged for an extensive display of photographs and books, but should very much like to widen the scope of the exhibition by including some personal relics of the campaign.

I wonder whether you would be willing to lend us anything like a map or notebook you used at the time, an original order of the day or signal, or else a trophy captured from the enemy? I know that this sort of exhibit would have a special appeal to the cadets, for whose instruction the exhibition is primarily being organised.

If you are able to help us in this way, I will arrange collection and return. All items will be insured, the Library building is secure, and, unless too large, exhibits will be placed inside locked show-cases.

Sure enough, Monty agreed in principle, and invited Peter Young to visit him at Isington Mill on the following Friday, 13th November, to select suitable items for exhibition.

'You'd better come too,' said Peter.

'But I'm not invited.'

'Oh! that doesn't matter. It was *your* idea. Anyway, you can come as my chauffeur!'

'In that case we'd better go in *my* car.'

'All right. Then I'll give you lunch.'

On this 50-50 basis we set off and lunched at Crondall. On the way Peter did impersonations of the Field-Marshal, in particular his pronunciation of an R rather like a W. Peter was laughing so much that I said: 'You must be careful or you'll find yourself imitating him when we get there. Or else he'll sound so much like your impersonation that we shall both explode with laughter. I certainly shan't be able to keep a straight face!'

We reached Isington Mill at half past two. A young woman, who seemed to be foreign, opened the front door and said: 'The Field-Marshal is upstairs.' We left our coats and followed her to the first floor. She knocked on the door straight in front and we entered a large sitting-room-cum-study having large windows at each end. Peter made the introductions and we shook hands.

Montgomery was dressed in a dark pullover and trousers, black shoes without laces, a dark brown shirt and faded blue tie with white dots. He looked very well, and had a good colour.

The first ten minutes of conversation were distinctly sticky, with Peter mentioning wartime names and trying, with patchy success, to find common ground. We appeared to be making very little headway.

Then, quite suddenly, Monty said: 'Well, sit down. Sit down.'

The atmosphere relaxed. I felt we had been accepted and were no longer 'on trial', so to speak. As Peter remarked later: 'From that moment on we were home and dry.' This was absolutely true: the Field-Marshal was, for the remainder of our visit, friendly and forthcoming.

Montgomery described a pre-D-Day row with Churchill (who, he said, was now quite senile and not expected to see ninety-one). Winston, in the belief that Monty was not taking enough *bayonets* to Normandy, drove down to Headquarters near Portsmouth* and wanted to discuss it with the Staff. Montgomery refused permission. Afterwards Churchill remarked to the staff officers a trifle peevishly, 'I wasn't allowed to talk to you.'

After nearly an hour he took us outside and across the gravel drive to the hangar and showed us the three caravans. The first, made in Italy, had been captured at Beda Fomm in 1941 and had belonged to General 'Electric Whiskers' Bergonzoli†. The second, which had belonged to General

---

* Broomfield House. King George VI lunched there on 22nd May 1944. See Montgomery's *Memoirs*, p 238.

† General Annibale Bergonzoli, nicknamed 'Electric Whiskers' because of his bristly beard which he parted in the centre, commanded the Italian garrison in Bardia. He escaped on foot to Tobruk, there took the last plane to Derna, was eventually captured by O'Connor's force on 7th February 1941, near Beda Fomm, south of Benghazi.

Messe and contained a bath, had portraits on the walls of Rommel, in colour, of Field-Marshal Model,* an awful looking thug with his cap at an angle and wearing an eyeglass – 'Dweadful fellow!' said Montgomery; Kesselring's much pleasanter face under a bald, domed brow; and two of von Rundstedt, whom Montgomery praised as a high-class professional.

Outside this caravan was the wooden board which the Field-Marshal had planted at the spot where the Germans surrendered on Lüneburg Heath, between Hamburg and Hanover. It had been removed the very first night, he said, so he sent for the Bürgermeister and told him that if the board was not back by nine o'clock the following morning he would have him shot. 'I could too . . . there'd have been a bit of a wow in the Commons, but still . . .'. The board was returned, and thereafter the Bürgermeister always had it watched by a German Home Guard.

These two caravans were 'booty'. Montgomery had them for life, but afterwards they were due to be given to the Imperial War Museum. The third, he explained, was his own. Made by the British Caravan Company, it had accompanied him from Normandy to the Baltic. The caravan walls were covered with maps showing the situation in Germany just after the surrender on 4th May 1945. Peter Young noted the 1st Commando Brigade up at Neustadt, the Canadians in Holland, the Welch Regiment in the Ruhr, the Scots Greys up against the Russians, and 400,000 German prisoners-of-war at the base of the Schleswig-Holstein peninsula. Montgomery described how everything had

* Walther Model commanded in Russia a panzer division, a corps, an army, and three different army groups before being sent to France to take over Army Group B.

broken down. The German troops up against the Russian Army had wanted to surrender to him *en masse*, but this he would not permit, although the surrender of individual Germans was allowed.

Montgomery had framed in his caravan a quotation from 'My Dear and Only Love' by James Graham, Marquis of Montrose:*

> He either fears his fate too much,
>   Or his deserts are small,
> That puts it not unto the touch
>   To win or lose it all.

Peter Young asked the Field-Marshal whether he knew the previous four lines of the stanza. He said he did not, so Peter recited them:

> Like Alexander I will reign
> And I will reign alone;
> My thoughts shall evermore disdain
> A rival on my throne.

The caravan hangar, he told us, had been made in Australia as a gift, and sent over piece by piece. We noticed that, besides the caravans, it contained a store of apples, several drop maps (mounted on canvas and rolled up) for lectures, and his grandchildren's tricycles.

Rain had been falling hard all the afternoon and it was getting dark when we left Isington. As we were stowing loan exhibits into my car, Montgomery spoke of a recent talk with

---

* After an exciting career, this military commander and poet was hanged in Edinburgh in 1650, aged 38.

Harold Wilson, whom he liked. 'Vewy capable.' The Field-Marshal thought the Tories needed a change or a rest and had 'wun out of ideas'.

Peter managed to persuade Monty to give him personally the signed original of a large map which we found rolled up in the hangar and which showed the location of all his headquarters from Alamein to Lüneburg. Some time back the Staff College at Camberley had produced for him a new version of the map, far better designed and lettered, so Monty made no difficulty about parting with the battered original.

As we drove back to his home at Yateley Peter was almost shaking with excitement, more so than I had ever seen him before. I too felt very elated after our encounter, but I expected Peter to be less stirred than I was. After all, he had led a commando brigade at the age of twenty-nine, had fought in many tough raids and battles, and had won the DSO and the MC with two bars.

We had tea chez Young and told his wife Joan all about our successful sortie, showing her the 'loot'. I returned to Sandhurst for dinner in the officers' mess.

Afterwards I was working in my two-room flat in one of the old Nissen huts on the hill above the RMA hospital when I heard a clatter of boots outside. Someone knocked on my door, and the guard commander appeared, in uniform.

'You're wanted on the telephone, sir.'

I ran down to the Mess, wondering what on earth was the matter. Was it an urgent message from my home in Mill Hill? Had my elderly mother been taken ill? No, I was to telephone Brigadier Young at once.

'Ah, B-J. You'd hardly left when our fwiend wang up. He wants you to wing him this evening.' He did not know what it was all about, but he gave me Monty's telephone number. I rang.

Monty answered in person. 'Bentley 3126.'

'Oh! it's Antony Brett-James speaking, sir. Brigadier Young said I was to ring you.'

'That's right. Can you come and have tea with me on Monday? I have a proposition to discuss which may interest you . . . Right then. I'll expect you at four!'

Thus a meeting was arranged, or so we thought.

However, on the Monday morning messages buzzed round Sandhurst. Field-Marshal Montgomery wanted to speak to 'Colonel Brett-James' on the telephone. Eventually I rang him and discovered that he was obliged to put off our meeting, as he was being admitted to hospital for an operation. He would be in touch with me later. It so happened that I too was taken ill and went home to Mill Hill for several days. While I was there the telephone rang. The local post office was on the line — 'Is that Colonel Brett-James? I have a telegram for you from Field-Marshal Montgomery.'

I don't know where Monty got the idea of my rank, since I had never risen above captain during the war and had no recollection of mentioning any rank to him. Indeed, I was employed as a civilian. The telegram read: 'Can you visit me an afternoon this week any time after 2 pm for a talk.' He was in King Edward VII Hospital for Officers: I knew from the newspapers that he had undergone a prostate gland operation in 'Sister Agnes'. The telegrams office said it was reply paid, so what reply did I wish to send? I could not decide on the spur of the moment, and wasn't sure whether I was fit enough to travel to London. I said I would telephone the hospital and arrange a meeting.

This all took place on 23rd November.

After lunch I rang the hospital and was put through to the sister. I asked her to give the Field-Marshal a message to say that I proposed to visit him two days later at three o'clock.

'Just a moment, sir. I think the Field-Marshal would like to speak to you himself.'

A moment's pause, then I heard the well-known metallic voice:

'When are you coming to see me?'

'Would Wednesday afternoon at three be convenient, sir?'

'Yes, fine. Expect you then.'

All very brisk and businesslike.

III

Wednesday, 25th November 1964
I arrived at King Edward VII Hospital in Beaumont Street at three o'clock and was shown up to the floor where Field-Marshal Montgomery had a room. The matron, Miss Saxby, took me in. I shook his hand. He was propped up in bed, wearing a dressing-gown. A profusion of flowers, books and magazines were on his left side towards the window. I stood at the foot of the bed. He handed me a document and said: 'Read that first.' I read a short account of the concept for a book on war which he had been commissioned to write. As far as I could gather, the book was to cover the period from earliest times until the present day and would be a blend of history and Montgomery's thoughts on war and soldiering and generalship.

I felt him waiting for me to finish reading something that he must have known almost by heart. He then explained that the firm of George Rainbird would produce the book and handle the editorial side, and that Collins would actually publish it. He was enlisting the services of a young research team who would work in London. In addition he needed someone experienced who would be an independent adviser, would help him plan the contents of the book, and would comment on each chapter as it was written.

'Do you know Fweddie de Guingand?'* he asked
suddenly. I had not met him, but knew his book *Operation
Victory* and was well aware that he had been Montgomery's
Chief of Staff from 1942 until the end of the war in Europe.

'Well, I need someone rather like that. A sort of Chief of
Staff for this project. Would you be prepared to undertake
the job?'

I was surprised, flattered and nonplussed by this proposal.
I fenced for time by enquiring how much work it would
entail and how long it would last. I added that of course my
work at Sandhurst must come first. This he accepted and he
gave me some idea of how long the task might last. I was still
hesitating when he rapped out:

'How much would you want? What sort of fee?'

I had absolutely no idea. He seemed to require an instant
reply, almost as though I had been calculating a reasonable
fee throughout the past week. Tentatively I suggested £500.

At once he said: 'Oh, I'll double that.'

It was arranged that I should set to work on a Table of
Contents, and this I did.

I had often heard what an exacting taskmaster the
Field-Marshal could be, and suspected that he might prove
very difficult to work for. After the war so many waspish
stories had circulated about him, mostly showing him in a
displeasing light. I disliked the way in which he had sacked
various subordinate commanders. I found unpalatable his

---

* Major-General Sir Francis de Guingand (1900-79) was Chief of Staff
  to Montgomery when commander of Eighth Army and 21st Army
  Group. His account of his wartime experiences, *Operation Victory*,
  appeared in 1947.

shabby and ungenerous treatment of his splendid chief of staff, General de Guingand, at the end of the war.

In particular I resented his disparagement of Auchinleck. Like everyone else who was fortunate enough to serve with the Indian Army – and I had been privileged to do this for the last three years of the war – I admired *that* field-marshal and felt affection for him as a human being. He had been kind to me; we had lunched together on half a dozen occasions in London; he had invited me to write an account of the Indian Army in the Second World War. Alas! I had been too busy with a full time job to accept, though I should dearly have liked to undertake the task. The 'Auk' felt a special sense of gratitude to the 5th Indian Division which had suffered grievous loss in the Desert battles of June and July 1942, when failure and retreat had been followed by ferocious fighting in the embryo defence line at Alamein to hold back and defeat the exultant Axis troops under Rommel's command. Later, in Burma, Auchinleck's own regiment, the 1st/1st Punjab, had been one of the bulwarks of our division, and after the war the 'Auk' had been a frequent and immensely welcome guest of honour at our reunion dinners. Montgomery had never been invited.

So all in all I could not describe myself as 'a Monty man'. Certainly at Sandhurst we studied with the cadets his battle of Alamein in detail, and we analysed D-Day and the Normandy campaign. As for the Arnhem failure, Monty had admitted in his *Memoirs* that he had not secured the final bridgehead and that he had made a bad mistake by underestimating the difficulties of opening up the approaches to Antwerp. Yet in his book *Normandy to the Baltic* he had claimed that the Arnhem operation was a ninety per cent success. This struck me as quite untrue.

On another score I was very conscious that my knowledge of the history of war was extremely patchy. I had not studied the subject at university, nor even history. Modern languages had been my field. I had never learnt so much so fast as I had done since joining the staff at Sandhurst at the end of 1961, sometimes only an hour or two ahead of the officer cadets I was teaching. As we began with Marlborough's campaigns, warfare in ancient times and in the Middle Ages and in Asia was largely unfamiliar ground. I realized that if I were to help the Field-Marshal properly I should have to read widely and work extremely hard. However, it was an exciting challenge.

I wondered how long I would last. Several friends and colleagues said helpfully: 'You just don't know what you're taking on.' This was certainly true, though not in the way they meant. If they were suspicious or cynical and I felt mildly apprehensive, we were wrong. Montgomery, while impatient to get back work he had sent out, was to prove reasonable, considerate, and prepared to listen. Provided I could accept his egocentricity, his wry humour, his occasionally schoolboyish attitudes, he was friendly, welcoming and very kind.

On 30th November, back at Sandhurst, I received another telegram which read: 'Not leaving hospital until 9th December so post table of content here = Field Marshal Montgomery.' This time I was correctly addressed as a Lecturer in Military History and not as a colonel!

I worked hard on the table of contents, which had the benefit of suggestions from Peter Young, and posted the result to Montgomery in hospital. In acknowledging this he wrote: 'I have been studying it most carefully and it is a very useful guide for the Producer and Publishers – and for the research team.'

He confirmed that he was going home to Isington Mill on the 9th 'for a quiet life.' He wanted to have a further talk before he set off on a six-weeks' sea voyage to South Africa. 'Could you come over to my home one afternoon after your term ends? If so, on what date?'

At this stage we were on 'Dear Brett-James . . . Yrs sincerely' terms. I arranged to visit Isington on 14th December, and was invited to tea at four o'clock.

Monday, 14th December 1964

Monty began by telling me that he wanted to pull me in as an assistant more than he had originally envisaged. I guessed that he was not feeling very strong after leaving hospital and consequently needed more help. Then he said: 'That figure we mentioned. I'll double it again.' With great consideration he offered to pay the fee in four instalments, spread over two years. My head was in a whirl at mention of all this money. How did one assess the amount of work involved? How long did he reckon the writing of the book would take? 'A year and a half.' I told him about my work at Sandhurst and my own writing projects. I also mentioned the likelihood that I would be ordered to lecture in Hong Kong, Malaya and Singapore for five weeks during August and September to officers preparing to sit the Staff College and Promotion examination.

He immediately wanted to know details. 'Who organises this? . . . Presumably you get paid?' Did I talk to officers out there, or could they be brought back to England for the purpose? I explained that commanding officers found it hard enough to release their captains for such courses, so these had to be local, though officers in Borneo were in fact flown to

27

Singapore to attend. No allowance could be made for the hot climate when they sat the examination in December. In 1963 I had done a similar lecture tour – to Malta, Tripoli and Cyprus, so I did 'know the form', as Monty put it, and I could answer his question.

'With all your other commitments, are you prepared to take on this job?'

The moment he put the question straight at me, with a kind though determined look in his piercing blue eyes, I said, 'Yes, I am. Definitely. It will be extremely interesting.' Thus I confirmed the provisional acceptance already given to him in hospital.

At this point the housekeeper came in. 'Did you ring, sir?' 'No, I didn't ring. Could it be Mr Westwood? He's bringing me some stamps.' She left the room.

Monty talked next about his sea trip to enjoy some sunshine for six weeks. He would get off at Durban and again at Cape Town. 'I used to go to Switzerland,' he added as an afterthought.

He asked me where I'd been at school. Mill Hill, I replied. 'Oh yes, of course. I was at St Paul's sixty years ago. I went there in 1902.' When he came home from Australia he was too old to go to his father's old school, Harrow. From St Paul's he had passed straight into Sandhurst, whereas in those days most young officers-to-be went first to a crammer's.

We talked of the book, which, in his view, would be read by a lot of people who knew nothing about the subject. So in Chapter 1 he aimed to explain the main things that are common to all wars. 'I imagine the average reader will be what I call the present generation.'

I suggested that from a general reader's point of view, some of the chapters at the end – on factors like communications, transport and generalship which go right through warfare – would be the most fruitful, rather than giving a purely chronological survey.

The housekeeper brought in tea on a tray and placed it on a low table in front of Monty, who was on a sofa facing the fireplace, while I sat in an armchair between him and the door.

She said to the Field-Marshal: 'It was Mr Shelford, sir. With a brace of pheasants. He said to give you his very kind wishes, sir.'

Had he come to the front door? Yes, he came in a car.

She should give the pheasants to the butcher next morning.

'Yes, sir. They're beautiful birds.'

Monty talked about his research team, especially of Alan Howarth, 'an absolutely brilliant young historian' at King's College, Cambridge. Next June he would get first class honours in History. Alan's father, Tom Howarth, the High Master of St Paul's, had been one of Monty's liaison officers in North-West Europe. Friends had told Alan, referring to researching for Monty: 'You do this job or you're mad.' He was now going to choose his own team mate, because they would have to share a flat over George Rainbird's offices for eighteen months. Monty had insisted on this arrangement. 'I told him what he really wanted was a fellow who would devil for him at the British Museum.'

Monty poured out another cup of tea for us both. 'Have some more food.' When I enquired whether he was going to have anything at all to eat, he replied: 'No. I may have one piece of cake.'

The next step, he said, was to get my synopsis approved by Rainbirds. Then the boys could go ahead. The whole thing

29

was to start on the first of July, after the boys had left university – on that day they would begin work in London. Meanwhile I could be thinking about the book while skiing – I was off on 20th December to Igls in Austria.

He asked me where I lived and whether I had a house. When I told him I had part of a hutted flat up the hill behind the hospital at Sandhurst, he told me that he had once lived in The Terrace and, when at the Staff College, had occupied a hut. 'I got married when I was there, 1927.'* He wanted to know about my job, how long tenure I had, what sort of pension, how long I'd been on the staff there. Could I tell what background a boy came from, and whether the standard had changed in the three years since I had arrived at the RMA?

He went on to say that one could go up the Army in two ways. The best way was to be equally good on the staff and in command. He had spent sixteen years on the staff and then commanded.

'But I've commanded everything there is to command. I never missed a single position: platoon, company, battalion, brigade, division, army corps, army, group of armies. That's rare. It's the way to do it. You can't be seen off.'

When he had been a corps commander and had inspected battalions, several commanding officers had said: 'Well, of course, you wouldn't understand that, sir.'

What a ridiculous thing to say, in any case, was my view. The CO was simply asking for trouble.

Monty bemoaned the fact that half the boys at Sandhurst would never reach the rank of lieutenant-colonel. 'To get

---

* He was married on 27th July 1927 to Elizabeth Carver, widow of Captain O. Carver, RE. Elizabeth Montgomery died in 1937.

command of a regiment these days is very difficult,' he said. 'One bad thing against you and you're *out*.'

This prompted me to mention some of the officers who, at the outbreak of war, had not passed Staff College and were not recommended for command, yet the war had given some of them the chance to show their true mettle. I told Monty about one of these whom I had come to know and admire with affection after the war: Major-General Denys Reid. As a young officer with the Seaforth Highlanders in the First World War he was twice wounded at Thiepval and at Passchendaele, and had won the DSO and MC and bar. Then he transferred to the Indian Army and by 1939 was second-in-command of the 3rd/5th Mahratta Light Infantry as a major with no prospects. When the battalion first went into action against the Italians on the Sudan-Eritrea border, it did none too well. Denys took over the command, did brilliantly, and was promoted to lead a brigade. While commanding the Eighth Army's rearguard during the retreat after Tobruk fell in June 1942, he was captured. When he escaped from a prison camp in Italy and made his way back to the Allied lines, Alexander had a division waiting for him: the 10th Indian.

Monty was distinctly interested, though he had never met Denys Reid. He went on to say that, of course, a war helped a military career: he had twice been promoted on the battlefield. He was made a substantive lieutenant-general a week before the battle of Alamein began. 'So you can say that at the battle I was the junior lieutenant-general in the Army List. When the battle was over I was promoted full general and skipped the whole of the lieutenant-generals at one go. The whole lot!' He chuckled at the recollection, which he obviously relished.

After Normandy he was made a field-marshal,* so he skipped all the generals. 'That's war. You must be in the right place. It's a great mistake to be too senior at the beginning of a war. I was in a very dangerous position. I was a major-general. A good young colonel – you're not responsible. But if you are Wavell – out! Gort – out!'†

Reverting to the projected book, he said he would have to see what sort of generals there were. Some of them are no use at all, and he recalled the French expressions – their two sorts of general: 'First there is *le bon général ordinaire* – he's the general who is extremely good as long as someone tells him what to do. The other type is what the French call *le grand chef*. Now he is the general who knows what to do. All he wants is a broad directive.' He instanced 'Stonewall' Jackson as *un grand chef* who could act on his own.

I reminded Monty that Jackson had been accidentally shot by his own men at Chancellorsville in 1863. However, he could show in the book just how much Lee missed Jackson at Gettysburg.

'I've been all over there,' said Monty.

On my way back to Sandhurst I posted a letter for him at Farnham Post Office.

Ten days before he sailed for Durban in the *Edinburgh Castle* Monty wrote to let me know that it had been decided that the *History of Warfare* was to be 150,000 words or so, instead of the 250,000 originally anticipated. Consequently he had re-examined my Table of Chapters and produced a

---

* His promotion dated from 1st September 1944.

† Appointed C-in-C-Middle East in 1939, General Lord Wavell was relieved by Churchill after the failure of the Battleaxe desert offensive, despite his earlier successes. General Lord Gort, C-in-C of the British Expeditionary Force, was relieved by Dill after Dunkirk.

General Montgomery with Eighth Army

Montgomery with Churchill in North Africa

'Second Edition'. What did I think of it? He added that his publishers, Collins, had informed him of the length of his other books: *Memoirs*, 195,000 words, *The Path to Leadership*, 80,000, and *Three Continents*, 65,000.

Friday, 8th January 1965
Term had just begun at Sandhurst when I visited Isington Mill again. As I drove my Rover in through the open gates, Monty was outside in the garden, getting some fresh air. I had brought with me all the items he had been kind enough to lend for the D-Day exhibition. Among these were a Strube cartoon, a colour photo of James Gunn's portrait of Montgomery, a volume of operation orders, and the little book in which Winston Churchill used to write his impressions whenever he visited Monty's HQ – published under the title *Ten Chapters*. From the car boot I took the case of badges of all formations in 21st Army Group – this had been skilfully repaired by George Leach of the National Army Museum – and put it in the hangar, and certain items in one of the caravans.

In the hangar Monty told me he had been to London the day before to get final clearance from the doctors – a month after leaving hospital. Then he asked whether our exhibition had been a success. It had. He thought he had said we might keep the copy of *Ten Chapters*, but I assured him that this permission had referred to the map of all his wartime headquarters sites. I reminded him that as the Staff College had produced a new edition, he had said we, that is to say Peter Young, could keep the original. I fastened the 21st Army Group badge in the caravan with a drawing-pin, and put the Gunn portrait and Strube cartoon there too. Then we went into the house and upstairs to his study.

33

'I've been living indoors for three weeks,' said Monty cheerfully. 'For the first fortnight I didn't go out, because that was what the doctors told me.'

We always met for discussion and tea in the long room which, with windows at each end, served Monty as study and sitting-room. It was comfortable but crowded. Indeed, in some respects it resembled a museum of his wartime and post-war career. On shelves, tables and the mantelpiece stood framed photographs showing his staff at 21st Army Group Headquarters, King George VI and Monty, Smuts, Tito, Mao Tse Tung, Liddell Hart, and Karsh's portrait of Churchill. Other photographs, most of them signed, were of King George VI, Queen Elizabeth wearing the sash of the Order of the Garter, the Queen Mother, the Duke of Edinburgh, Princess Margaret, Princess Marina Duchess of Kent, King Haakon of Norway – this was framed in red with a gold-embossed crown on top – Field-Marshal Alexander, and Monty with the King in North Africa.

James Gunn's painting of Monty and his liaison officers at table in a tent adorned the wall beyond the Field-Marshal's desk; to its left hung a smaller oil of Monty's caravan parked on the edge of a field, with trees just behind.

The photograph to which Monty referred most frequently concerned the Victory Parade in London held on 8th June 1946. Monty, wearing battledress and beret, is seen standing in his open staff car and saluting King George VI as he passes the saluting base in the Mall. According to the Field-Marshal, no salutes were to be given, but he was having none of it.

'I wasn't going to pass my Sovereign and not salute,' he rapped.

Like many elderly men (he was born in 1887), he

appeared to derive reassurance, if not gleeful pleasure, from surviving his contemporaries. So every time he showed me this large framed photograph he would say: 'They're dying from the right!' On the royal dais stood King George VI, accompanied by Queen Elizabeth, Queen Mary, and Princesses Elizabeth and Margaret. On the right hand side, reading from the right, sat Field-Marshal Jan Smuts, Prime Minister of the Union of South Africa, then Mr Mackenzie King, Prime Minister of Canada – he wore top hat and morning clothes. Next to him sat first Mr Churchill and then Mr Attlee, the former and the recently elected Prime Ministers, both in morning dress adorned with medals.

To the left side of the dais, seated from right to left, were the three Chiefs of Staff: Admiral of the Fleet Lord Cunningham, Field-Marshal Lord Alanbrooke, and Marshal of the RAF Lord Portal. Next to him was Field-Marshal Lord Alexander, then the bulky figure of Field-Marshal Lord Wilson, followed by Admiral Lord Louis Mountbatten and General Sir Hastings Ismay, Chief of Staff to Churchill in his capacity as Minister of Defence.

It was to this front row that Monty referred when he used to say, in his clipped, decisive way: 'They're dying from the right.' In this claim he was not wholly accurate. True it is that when I first heard him say it Smuts and Mackenzie King had died in 1950, Churchill on 24th January 1965, and Attlee in October 1967. But by this time the sequence had been upset, for Cunningham and Alanbrooke had both died in June 1963, 'Jumbo' Wilson had departed this life on the last day of 1964, and Ismay had gone in December 1965. Alexander survived until June 1969 and Portal two years more. Mountbatten was murdered by the IRA while on holiday in Ireland, on 27th August 1979.

35

Historical value had been added to this photograph by the fact that Monty had persuaded King George VI, Queen Elizabeth, Queen Mary, Princess Elizabeth to autograph it. So too had Smuts, MacKenzie King – his signature had been pasted on, Churchill, whose autograph had faded, and C. R. Attlee. Beneath his staff car Monty had written in turquoise blue ink 'Montgomery of Alamein'.

Over the mantelpiece hung one of Churchill's paintings in oil. I asked about it.

'It's near Marrakesh. The Atlas Mountains.'

We discussed the book and the likely format Rainbird had in mind.

'If it's going to have biggish diagrams, it's got to be a biggish page. A biggish page.' This was a favourite verbal mannerism of the Field-Marshal, to repeat the last few words of a sentence.

Did I agree that 150,000 words was right for length? Yes, but one could not at this stage give oneself too rigid a blueprint. Up to 160,000 would be in order, but a complete rationing to 150,000 would be too hampering. Do publishers count the index in the length of a book? No, nor the preliminaries.

He repeated how brilliantly clever Alan Howarth was – 'brilliantly clever' – and how he was heading for a research studentship at Cambridge. He had chosen a medical student friend named Anthony Wainwright from London University to be his working partner and to share the flat. They had been at school together at Rugby. Monty had had Alan down to Isington and told him to prune the table of contents to about 25 chapters: as a result they had produced the typed pages which he had marked 'Second Edition' in red ink. I was now to produce the third and final version. I put in the caveat 'in so far as one can have anything final at this stage'.

Monty had in mind that the reader would have a short, one-page preface which would tell him to read Chapter 1 carefully; and in this first chapter he would find the things which really affect the military art. Did I agree? By and large I did, but I suggested that the chapter should be a general consideration, as seen by himself. It should be a book of Montgomery ruminating, drawing deductions and conclusions from events and personalities. He agreed it should not be a work of reference, and added:

'I suppose I'm the only person who has tried to write on war who has commanded everything from a platoon to a group of armies.'

I emphasised that the book must not be one that almost *any* historian could write. 'It's got to be a supreme commander who is writing the book.'

He wanted me to pick out from each period one or two battles for special study.

Monty had told Rainbird that he could break the story to the press once he, Monty, had left the country. That is, not before 15th January. Rainbird knew about the team: 'Me, and these two boys, and you. You're the backstop this end, *not* in London.' Completely separate from the Rainbird office. I asked what I was to say if approached by any newspaper about the project.

'You simply say: "I've been asked by the Field-Marshal to help".'

'And if they ask for details of the nature of the book?'

'Nothing. You can say: "It's early days yet. We don't start work until July. It's still in the planning stage".'

He said he would have the two boys to Isington every week

to discuss the next week's work. He would make them both members of the London Library, and they could do the job in less than eighteen months. Alan Howarth had suggested they produce their research in the form of draft chapters. Monty seemed delighted at this notion: he could change the draft, put it into his own language.

'They give you a fact,' I stressed, 'and you turn it into an idea.' There being no further points to discuss that day, Monty showed me round his home. First what he called his flat, with the sitting-room in which we had been talking. Out of it opened two bedrooms, one of them really his dressing-room. He pointed to the servants' quarters – three bedrooms and their own bathroom. And downstairs the kitchen, larder, their sitting-room and all the rest.

He led me up to the top floor – a similar flat to his own, with an even better view.

'It was really designed when my boy* was at Winchester, so he could bring his friends.'

Now it would be very convenient for the research team every weekend.

As we went down the stairs I noticed, on the landing, a picture of Napoleon.

'Right, well you push off now.' Monty always had a deft, firm way, quite kindly, of bringing any meeting to a close. He accompanied me outside, and he waited to close the gates behind my car.

*

By the time Monty agreed to what he entitled 'Second Edition' the concept of the book had altered in several

* David Montgomery, who became the 2nd Viscount in 1976.

respects. Our main task would be to indicate what was significant in the outstanding generals, wars, battles and technological developments in the history of warfare. Much of the book's value would lie in its unique, subjective approach, presenting 'the views and judgements of a soldier who has made a life study of the profession of arms and who has himself taken part in active operations in the field. . . .'

Because of the reduction in length, the table of contents had been pruned and the new outline embraced twenty-seven chapters.

The Field-Marshal, having already written the first chapter, decided to tackle the last six chapters so that these could be in the hands of the research team when they started work in July. They would have a solid background against which to research and a pointer to where they were going.

Montgomery had decided that it would be unsound at this stage to draw up a definitive 'blueprint' for each chapter. The contents must remain tentative and subject to modification, and many of the details set down were primarily for the guidance of himself and the research team, to serve as yardsticks or as points of departure for comment, comparison and reflection.

He declared a preference for the title *Montgomery on War*, implying that he was merely giving his views on war, whereas *A History of Warfare* would commit us to produce a detailed and chronological history and lay us open to criticism that much had been left out.

The first five battles for which I had to provide detailed plans, as accurate as research could make them – none too easy for the very early encounters – were Kadesh in 1288 BC, where the Egyptians beat the Hittites; Gaugamela where Alexander the Great overthrew Darius and the Persian

Empire in 331 BC; the naval battle of Salamis in 480 BC; Hannibal's defeat by Scipio Africanus in 202 BC at Zama; and Crécy in 1346 AD.

The list of battles changed from time to time; names were struck out and even put back again, and several substitutions were made. Hastings, 1066, was added for one. The only typed letter Monty sent me, dated 11th February 1966, confirmed this trend and the plans still required at that stage.

At one time we did make certain changes in the list of battles, and the table of contents got altered occasionally! The remaining battles for which we shall need maps from you are now as follows – and these are now firm:

Sea Battles		Land Battles	
Lepanto	1571	Crécy	1346
Off Portland	1653	Kyushu	1587
Trafalgar	1805	Ramillies	1706
Tsushima	1905	Leuthen	1757
Jutland	1916	Valmy	1792
Midway	1942	Austerlitz	1805
		Gravelotte	1870
		Tannenberg	1914
		Meiktila	1945

You will notice that we have put back Trafalgar (which had been removed) and brought in Jutland – because it was considered the naval aspect of warfare was not being given adequate representation. We now have one sea battle in each World War.

You will also notice that I have thrown out Dien Bien Phu. I have included in Chapter 24 (*The Cold War*) some remarks about the British War against the Chinese guerillas in Malaya during the Templer regime in 1952/54 – also remarks about the French War in Vietnam 1946/54 which ended with the loss of Dien Bien Phu in 1954 – also a note about the present American War in Vietnam. These Cold War activities are worth studying, and comparing, but require no maps.

Even this 'firm' list was altered as the months went by. Lepanto was discarded because the text was insufficiently clear. Monty substituted Breitenfeld (1631) for Off Portland, which he considered 'too messy for a diagram', and Blenheim, with Marlborough's March to The Danube (1704), for Ramillies. Valmy, Trafalgar and Kyushu were also deleted, the first because it was little more than 'a tremendous cannonade'. Tsushima was dropped later still.

IV

Monty sailed for South Africa in mid-January. I received a letter from him dated Cape Town 11-2-65 on RMS *Edinburgh Castle* Union-Castle Line paper: he was due home on 26th February; he had written Chapter 1; could I come to tea on the following Sunday, the 28th, at 4.00 p.m. – and bring with me the completed third edition of the Table of Contents?

Sunday, 28th February 1965

Monty handed me Chapter 1 to read there and then. 'I wrote this at Port Elizabeth where it was very hot. I didn't go ashore.' He had given it to two civilians on board; they were very pleased and of course wanted to read the completed book. I handed him my third edition of the Table of Contents: this kept to the twenty-seven chapters laid down in the second edition, but went into much greater detail.

He told me George Rainbird had, while lunching at Isington, discussed the title, and he too wanted to call it *Montgomery on War*. For the time being he called it *On War* by Montgomery.

He then talked about the after-effects of his prostate operation. He had met several men on board ship who had also had this operation and he used to ask them on deck in the morning.

'They reckon it's six months before you really begin to feel that you can lead a normal life. And nine months before you are 100%. They all said the same thing: after nine months you'll be a completely new person. But you musn't get tired. You can do what you like after six months, but the moment you get tired, stop. That's what I do.'

He had to sit at the captain's table.

'I don't like it, because it means you have to sit there till everyone's finished. If a person's a slow eater, there you've got to sit.'

He chuckled at this.

I asked him what he had done all day

'I never appeared before eleven o'clock. I had breakfast in bed. I took a huge double cabin for myself – got to pay for the other bunk, of course. There's the auction sweep on the day's run. Coming back I was £25 up – enough to pay for my tips. The afternoon is devoted to sleep.'

He left the ship at Durban – and stayed in an air-conditioned suite because the humidity was 90%. He had also got off at Cape Town and stayed with some very rich friends.

'I like to get out of England in January and February. You come back just now and it's a very important time in the garden. And the pruning is done.'

Anyhow, to be away for six weeks was enough, as he had still not caught up with the backlog of letters and bills. Having been in a temperature of 90°, he had to be careful on his return to Hampshire not to catch 'the father and mother of a cold.' He wore a very thick coat if he went outside.

The housekeeper brought in tea, while Monty told me

again that young Howarth was very clever – 'a brilliant historian' – and very independent, with his own ideas. Then he asked if the dates he had given for payment were suitable for my income tax. When I mentioned that the new increase of standard rate from 7s 9d to 8s 3d didn't begin till April, he took the point at once. It would be an advantage to have one payment before April, in March in fact. He altered his copy of the pencilled memo about payments.

He kept telling me to help myself to homemade buttered scones and jam, and to slices of Swiss Roll and jam sponge cake. 'I'm not a great eater,' he said.

Several times he blew his nose loudly. The clock chimed every fifteen minutes.

We talked of the book. He said the chapter on Secret Service and Intelligence could be written now, so I said the one about generalship could also. He suggested taking certain generals and looking at them to see in which category they fitted and how they did their stuff. How would that do? I replied that some could be dealt with as the book went along, while others could be picked out to illustrate his line of argument about generalship as a whole. He thought he would take what one looks for in generals – in command, in battle. He didn't want to go further back than Hannibal.

From time to time Monty punctuated the conversation with 'Will you have some more tea?' or 'Eat some more food.'

He'd have to write on whether war is an art or a science. He thought it was both:

'The art of war is putting the theory of your profession – the science – into practice. I don't believe you can really understand war unless you've done both – unless you've done both.'

Half the military writers had not practised the art, only

44

studied the theory. Like Liddell Hart*.

'I know him extremely well. Do you know him?'

Time and again Monty would mention a name, and ask me if I knew the man concerned. I had usually heard of him, or read his books, but very seldom knew the person. It was almost as if Monty felt he gained kudos by knowing such people, by having friends of their calibre. I felt it was likely to be the other way round: *they* got kudos by knowing Field-Marshal Montgomery.

This anxious desire to be known to have friends, and friends of long standing, was strange. He had fame, but he seemed to lack personal security. One suspected that any man who so emphatically proclaimed his friendships must feel that he had few intimate friends. He was essentially a lonely man, though outwardly at least he appeared not to mind. While part of him could be abrasive, egotistical and opinionated, the rest was kindly, simplistic and endearing. Certainly he was very human in his vanities, in his need to show me, for example, a new book by Arthur Bryant inscribed 'to our greatest since Wellington.'

It would have been more understandable if I had tried to build myself up in Monty's eyes by dropping a few names, but surely he, already a legend and firmly in history books, had no need to do this with me. But he did, time after time. So with Liddell Hart.

* Basil Liddell Hart, formerly Military Correspondent of *The Daily Telegraph* and of *The Times*, became a leading exponent of mechanised war and influenced reforms of the British Army when serving as personal adviser to Hore-Belisha, the War Minister, 1937-38. Besides books on Sherman, Foch, Scipio Africanus and T. E. Lawrence, Liddell Hart wrote histories of the First and Second World Wars, a History of the Tanks, and many other influential, thought-provoking works.

'He's a great friend of mine. I've known him for forty years. Now he's a great student of war, but he hasn't practised the art.'

I suggested that this was precisely what Monty himself had to offer in a unique way in this particular book. He agreed, and laughed when he added that somebody wouldn't like it if he said that you can't really understand war unless you've done both. I felt that one could get a pretty shrewd idea from memoirs and talk, but one couldn't know it *inside* oneself. Monty went on to say:

'I don't think you can understand the intense loneliness at times. You feel alone, naked.'

If you haven't held high command in war you don't really know how much you can leave to chance, and how much you can't. That, surely, was the *art* of war as against the science of war.

He mentioned Clausewitz*, so I told Monty he had served in the 1812 campaign on the Russian side. He, along with other Prussian officers, went across to that side when their king made a pact with Napoleon. Monty was in one of his typically staccato, clipped, question-barking moments. This sort of thing:

'He went to Moscow?'

I explained that Clausewitz served in the Russian Army as chief of staff to one of the corps.

'He was a German?'

I said there had been a number of Germans on the Russian side.

'So he's done both.'

---

* Karl von Clausewitz (1780-1831), Prussian general, whose writings were published after his death under the title *On War*, one of the most important and influential books on the theory of war ever written.

I suggested that Clausewitz had not actually held a field command. Monty countered this by stating that Clausewitz would have known the form, as de Guingand had. 'If you're chief of staff, you really know,' he remarked conclusively. Then he added that in modern times Slim had done both – 'He really knows what he's talking about in this game.'

I was delighted that Monty thought so highly of Slim, because I had served in his Fourteenth Army in Burma for two years, had the utmost confidence in his generalship, and thought him to be a very fine human being. His memoirs, *Defeat into Victory*, were exceptionally well written, and he was ready to admit his mistakes. By concentrating on Slim in the book, he could avoid mentioning himself. He laughed.

There was further talk about alterations to Table of Contents number 3, and notes he might add between now and July. He told me he had decided to take 'The Idea of Peace' section out of Chapter 27 and put it into an Epilogue. Should it be called 'The pattern that future wars are likely to take?' Should we stick our neck out a bit without making readers feel that the synopsis of all the other chapters was nonsense. He laughed at this, because I had already sounded a warning note that this might be the effect. He asked whether I would put in a sentence like: 'Until the future is more certain, the free world must hang together.' He said I could tackle Chapter 24, 'The Ethics of War', and then added that 'the boys' could have a go at all this; I must be prepared to comment.

I showed Monty a photograph from the Belgian periodical *Waterloo illustré* – the Field-Marshal being shown the battlefield from the top of the Lion Mound by an elderly local guide. He told me it was while he lived in Brussels. The officer beside him was a Canadian named Warren. When

Monty commanded South-Eastern Army before going to North Africa, the Canadians came under his command, so he said to General Andy McNaughton*: 'Now I must have a Canadian ADC as a link with your chaps.' The message went down to the divisions.

'No takers,' said Monty. 'Terrible chap!' He laughed. 'My reputation of getting rid of people who were quite useless on efficiency put them off.'

Finally one of the Canadian brigadiers was told: 'You've bloody well got to produce one.' All the battalions said they did not wish to provide an ADC. It was a last effort. Then this young officer, Warren, said he didn't mind. Again Monty chuckled.

When he flew off to Africa the Canadians remained in England, so Warren did too, but he rejoined Monty when the 1st Canadian Division moved to Sicily.

'He went right through to the end of the war. An awfully nice bloke. We became tremendous friends. I go and stay with him whenever I go to Canada. He's a very rich business man. Very able.'

Monty blew his nose.

He recalled how Warren first came to see him at his headquarters near Reigate. Monty was in bed with flu, so Warren, who had never seen him before, was shown into the bedroom and sat in a chair. As Monty explained:

'He expected to be interviewed about his military knowledge, instead of which I asked him about his family and his wife. He was amazed. I suppose he expected me to ask: "What are your views on platoon tactics?"' Monty

* General Andrew McNaughton commanded the Canadian Corps in Britain 1940-42, and then the First Canadian Army until his retirement in 1944 to become Canada's Minister of National Defence.

laughed at the memory.

'He went right through to the end – right through to the end'. Again that characteristic reiteration of the final words – emphatic and conclusive.

Then a typical dismissal. 'I don't think you want any more. You're quite happy.' He noted that I would be on holiday from 7th to 28th April.

*

During the next two weeks I posted him a number of suggestions, and received a short letter from Isington Mill dated 16-3-65 which read:

> I will do as you suggest about my habits of study prior to rising to high command. You say 'We know what Wellington and Napoleon read at various stages.' I, personally, do *not* know. Can you please send me this information.

I let him know that Napoleon took to Italy Guibert's *Essai général de tactique* and Bourcet's *Principes de la guerre des montagnes*; before going to Egypt in 1798 he read Raynal's *Histoire des deux Indes* and *Considérations sur la guerre actuelle des Turcs* by Volney. When he went to Egypt he ordered Bourrienne to buy books on Polybius, Peter the Great, Frederick the Great, Marlborough, Prince Eugene, Saxe, Luxembourg, Condé, Turenne and Charles XII, as well as a *Traité des fortifications* and an *Aide nécessaire pour l'artillerie*.

As for Wellington, he took to India a score of histories, accounts and memoirs of the country, Persian and Bengali grammars, Major-General Lloyd's *Reflections on the General*

Principles of War and his *War in Germany*, Saxe's *Mes Rêveries*, Dundas's *Cavalry Tactics*, Frederick the Great's *Histoire de la Guerre de Sept Ans* – and, above all, Caesar's *Commentaries*, from which he learnt much in India and on which he improved.

Four days later Monty wrote to say that he had lunched with the two researchers in London and would like us all to meet. Could I manage lunch on Friday, 2nd April, for a good discussion on how best to tackle the job. The date also suited my timetable, so I telephoned to say I would go.

On 29th March he sent me the Rainbird's staff's re-draft of his first chapter, 'The Nature of War', which they thought good. Did I agree? His letter went on:

> I had Oliver Leese* here this weekend. His comment was that Chapter 1 is too good, and that I have given away in it my whole philosophy on War! It is not necessary to read the book! He reckoned I should take something out of it and put it into Chapter 26 (Generalship).

He enclosed a new piece to be inserted in that chapter and told me he had removed one paragraph from Chapter 1. He had also decided that a short Preface was needed, and sent me a draft which we could discuss when I came to lunch.

Monty always addressed envelopes in his own hand: almost square envelopes, long ones, occasionally embossed with the royal coat of arms on the flap, pale blue envelopes bearing Carlton Hotel, Bournemouth on the back. Several letters came from Cape Town, bearing 12½c. Republic of

---

* Lieut.-General Sir Oliver Leese, former commander of XXX Corps under Montgomery in North Africa, and his successor in command of the Eighth Army in Italy.

South Africa stamps and an Air Mail label. Quite a number of large buff ON HER MAJESTY'S SERVICE envelopes arrived in the post, and one large envelope reached me with two green and white Post Office SPECIAL DELIVERY labels and 1s 10½d. worth of stamps affixed. The great majority of letters from Monty were postmarked Alton or Farnham, but occasionally it was London, Bournemouth-Poole, and on one occasion the House of Lords. Almost invariably he would intitial the bottom left hand corner of the envelope *M of A* or *From* M of A and once *From* M of Alamein – probably a habit left over from wartime censorship regulations. One morning when a letter came to my office at Sandhurst my colleague David Chandler looked at the address and, seeing the M of A, said quite seriously, 'What's that stand for? Ministry of Agriculture?'!

V

I lunched for the first time at Isington to meet the pair of London-based researchers of whom Monty had spoken so often: Alan Howarth and Anthony Wainwright. We got along very well together, discussing little except the book and how it was to be planned and written. Monty himself was a firm but benevolent host, incisive in style, often clipped in speech, but ready to listen to the ideas and suggestions, the objections and arguments which we sent shuttling across the lunch table. He seemed in high spirits and made mildly teasing jokes. We argued about the overall balance of the history and the way we might approach the numerous periods and themes. How much attention should be paid, for example, to warfare in Asia? Did Alan and Anthony need a short bibliography from me for every chapter? Had they any problems about those chapters which we had written already? Insofar as such matters could be agreed at this early stage, they were so, and the meeting was immensely helpful.

My chief memory of this occasion is the white paper napkins provided for each guest. In one corner had been printed in dark blue letters M of A. Monty explained that he had pinched the idea from Winston Churchill, who had his initials on similar napkins. I wondered what the Field-Marshal's ancestors portrayed along the wall, would have made of this harmless and engaging quirk.

At Monty's suggestion a meeting was arranged between George Rainbird and myself in London 'in connection with the book he is writing for us *Montgomery on War*, and, as I understand it, you are acting as his historical reader and adviser'. We met at 11.30 on 5th May and had a very valuable talk about the book and its outline and all the research to be done. He kindly sent me a set of General Fuller's* *Decisive Battles of the Western World* in three volumes, as I had asked for this vital reference work for the task ahead.

As the other director most closely involved with Monty's project, John Hadfield, was away in America on 5th May, he invited me to lunch with him on 2nd June. I, meanwhile, had met George Rainbird again one evening at dinner, when he asked me to look at Monty's first chapter because he was not happy about the opening paragraph. Could it be more dramatic? It was likely to be the first page to be read, particularly by critics, and therefore had an importance out of all proportion to the rest of the book. Would I turn the idea over in my head and discuss it when I met John Hadfield?

In sending me Chapter 27 on 20th May 1965, Monty wrote:

I was visited here yesterday by George Rainbird and Hadfield. We cleared up many points, including your

---

* Major-General J. F. C. Fuller, a leading proponent of armoured warfare and an influential writer on war, past and future. His nickname 'Boney' alluded to Bonaparte, as he was small but very forceful.

place in the set-up – about which they are now in no doubt!!

On one point there is deadlock: the portrait of myself. I adhere to my decision that I should be shewn in uniform; Rainbird wants me in plain clothes. I am under the impression that Hadfield agrees with me although he didn't like to say so in front of his boss!

Five days later he wrote me a note to accompany a revised version of his piece about Napoleon:

I have decided to have nothing to do with the Dutch artist. His style of portraiture does not appeal to me. Poor George!

Tuesday, 29th June 1965
I went again to Isington Mill for tea. As usual Monty was upstairs in his sitting-room. 'The two boys move into their château today,' he announced briskly.

They were lunching with him in London next day and he had ordered them down for the weekend. His idea was that they should go through the seven chapters we had written. It was essential for them to know the background. He would sit them down and go through each chapter. Did I think this was the best way?

'They must know how I write. They've got to understand that in anything I write the opening sentence is very important.'

I said this would give him an opportunity of stating exactly what he required, with a text in front of him, and it would give the boys a chance to ask questions and clear up misunderstandings. Would they have read the chapters

before the weekend? Monty was not sure. Certainly they had
received them, because whenever a chapter was typed, I
received a copy, Rainbird got one, the boys had one, he
himself had a copy.

Then Monty enquired whether I approved of the chapter
he had written, 'The Changing Ethics of War', based on my
material. I had left it in sections, which was how he wanted it,
and he had tried to make a story of it, adding his own
conclusions. 'The interesting thing will be whether the
historians agree with them.'

Liddell Hart had been to see him the day before. Did I
know him? he asked me again. Unfortunately I had never
met him, though I explained how two of his books, *The Ghost
of Napoleon* and *The Fog of War*, were chosen as part of my
college prize for getting a first class in the modern languages
prelims at Cambridge in 1940. Predictably Monty then said
again:

'Oh! he's a great friend of mine. Known him for years.'

Liddell Hart and his wife had been on their way to see old
Lady Lloyd George at Churt. She wanted Liddell Hart to
advise her about writing her memoirs.

Suddenly he switched the conversation to a new book by
'Boney' Fuller, *Julius Caesar*.

'Do you know "Boney" Fuller?'

Again I had to say 'no', though I had read several of his
books. Monty commented that some fellows like Fuller and
Charles Broad* – 'do you know him?' – had missed getting
right up. 'They got up near the top and then mucked it up.
They didn't get there.' I don't know why Monty went off at

* Lieut.-General Sir Charles Broad, who retired in 1942. His last post
  was GOC-in-C Eastern Army, India.

this particular tangent, but the implication was inevitably that he *had* got to the very top.

By this time I had rung the bell and the housekeeper had brought tea on a tray. From time to time Monty would interrupt the conversation about personalities or the book to say things like: 'You eat what you like. Sandwiches, scones . . .' or I would say: 'Can I bother you for the milk?' after he had refilled my cup from the pot.

While I was munching hot buttered scones, very good ones too, he asked if these were served at Sandhurst. I told him that we had them once in three months, maybe, and usually warm and rather chunky in texture.

'Do you have tea in the mess? On a table?' He always wanted to have details of Sandhurst life.

'Do eat some food,' he would urge. 'Won't you have anything?'

I would reply, feeling I was helping myself rather greedily. 'No, I'm not a big eater. *You* eat it.'

Perhaps ten minutes later Monty would say: 'Have some more food.' By this time I could only refuse with thanks, having done very well by the tea.

I need not have worried about appearing greedy. On one occasion a plate of delicious sandwiches appeared on the tray beside the cake. 'Have another sandwich,' Monty said a few minutes later. 'If you eat the whole lot she'll be very pleased,' referring to the housekeeper.

Talk reverted to the book and 'the boys'. Monty felt they must have a programme of work. Start work at nine o'clock and work all the morning. In the afternoon they could walk in Hyde Park or play squash at the Queen's Club, and then do the evening stint.

'They must have a routine,' he said with emphasis. 'Don't

you agree with that? Otherwise they'll go all haywire.'

I agreed with doing a really good stint both morning and evening; then one could relax in the afternoons; but Monty seemed to contradict himself, one moment saying that he couldn't work the boys twelve hours a day or they'd go mad, and the next moment stating that in winter they might decide to work all day, as there would be no point in going out in pouring rain. He thought they could bring books home from the libraries and that Alan would probably send Anthony to dig stuff out of the British Museum.

George Rainbird had written to tell Monty that on Alan's *strong* recommendation he had engaged a very good secretary. Monty laughed:

'I don't mind as long as she's good! She can make their tea!'

I told Monty I had brought with me a tentative list of major battles since 1708, and would let him have a skeleton of the three battles to be studied in Chapters 2 and 3 before the end of term in late July. He wanted to know what form the skeleton would take and was interested to see if the boys could write up a battle once I had produced the framework. I said I did not think we should give just a straight detailed account of each key battle in the book. Better to pick out features which made a battle typical of its period or typical of its commander. So Monty decided that I should say why each battle had been selected – and give the salient points. I stressed that we should go for what was typical rather than saying that a battle was a particularly decisive one.

He was undecided whether he should write about the battles or whether the boys should do it. We must be careful to ensure that the book did not contain different styles of writing. 'Everyone knows how I write. We've got to be very careful.' Undoubtedly his style is distinctive, even idiosyncratic. I suggested that besides a writer's actual use of language there was his approach to the subject, his method of tackling it. Monty agreed with this, and said he must, in going through the seven chapters so far typed, make the boys see how *he* approached a subject. That would be very important for them.

I put forward my view that in submitting a chapter, Alan and Anthony should not make it too finished a job. They should not do all the dovetailing of sections, then it would be easier for him to make the material his own. If he were to receive too polished a product, he would find much greater difficulty in unravelling the chapter. He would have to do more rewriting and re-hacking. Let them end the page whenever they came to the close of a section. Monty thought this a good point.

Next we discussed battles. He had been thinking it would be interesting to put in one like Dien Bien Phu.* I had already done just this. Had I read Jules Roy's book† on the subject? No. 'By Jove! As an example of vacillation – dreadful! And the incompetence of command. Cogny,** of course, was with me. An intriguer of the first water!' Monty

---

* A plan later discarded. See letter on p.40-41.

† *The Battle of Dien Bien Phu*, translated by Robert Baldick (1963). On 7th May 1954 French forces were compelled to surrender after this fierce battle in northern Vietnam.

** René Cogny (1904-1968), an artillery officer, was taken prisoner in 1940, escaped from a Stalag in 1941, joined the Resistance, and was arrested in 1943, being deported to Buchenwald after six months' imprisonment at Fresnes. He accompanied General de Lattre de Tassigny to Indo-China. There he commanded the 2nd Tonkin Infantry Division, and later took command of all armed forces in Tonkin. A giant in stature, Cogny loved ceremonial, and could be touchy and violent.

laughed. 'I know him very well.' Dien Bien Phu brought out all the lessons of the 'mucking up' by the politicians.

More battles, Leuthen, Valmy, Austerlitz, perhaps Salamanca. When Monty demurred at the last name because we must keep away from too much British, I said we had very few British battles, and one should make the point that Napoleon always underestimated Wellington. Chancellorsville. Gravelotte-Saint Privat. Mukden. Tsushima.

What did I feel about including the battle of Tannenberg for 1914? We could say that everyone is fed up with the mud and blood of the Western Front slogging-match, so let's have a look at another battle.

For the Second World War I had proposed Sedan, to illustrate the superb German technique of Blitzkrieg, and Alamein, as a turning-point battle. Monty felt we should *not* include Alamein. Too much had already been written. Mareth would be better – 'a terrific battle'. He believed we needed one battle only.

I mentioned the huge slogging-matches of the Pacific from island to island, especially Okinawa – the casualties at Alamein were trifling compared to what went on at Okinawa. I also said that Meiktila in central Burma was a master-stroke of manoeuvre and deception, part of the Fourteenth Army getting right round behind the Japanese and throttling their lines of communication to the Irrawaddy defence line.

Monty responded at once to the idea of a Far East, Burma campaign battle.

'We shall be criticised if we stick to the West. That'll please the Burma people. Were you at Meiktila? I'm all against Alamein.'

He wanted to know the date of Meiktila, and who

succeeded Slim in command of Fourteenth Army, and whether Oliver Leese had gone home before Meiktila. Could we deal with a battle in a single page, as he had done with the battle of the Nile, by not going into detail? We must indicate the salient points of each battle, the results, and the commanders – 'What sort of guys they were.' Monty often used the word 'guy' – a favourite expression.

He told me he was going to South Africa again on 26th January for about six weeks, and would spend a fortnight in a very nice château at Cape Town. He had taken a large cabin with sofas and tables and air-conditioning. 'The funny thing about life on a boat is the lack of time. You get up late, and the morning goes, what with the sweep on the ship's run. In the afternoon it's damned hot and one wants a sleep. When it's cool one walks about the deck and watches the games.' As a result, he would only be able to do a limited amount of work on the book. He would go very carefully through the seven chapters.

VI

I arrived at 5.15, well after tea, and spent an hour with
Monty, who began by telling me that because Alan Howarth
was 'absolutely brilliant' – I was getting mildly irritated at
this repeated praise – and Anthony was a very good digger,
and they had an efficient secretary, he would not want me as
much as he thought he would. 'I wanted you when I was
alone.'

Now he wanted me to produce diagrams of all the battles
studied in detail based on the narrative in their text. Kadesh,
Gaugamela, Salamis and Zama were the first four. He no
longer wished me to produce notes on the battles. The boys
must do this. They were quite capable of doing so.

He handed me a carbon copy of the first four chapters;
Chapter 4 had been finally typed the night before. Monty
explained that in London Alan did some of the research,
Anthony did some, and so did Miss Bunney, the secretary.
At a certain date Alan called in all the research material and
then he wrote it into notes for Monty. These were sent to
Isington and Monty wrote the first draft of the next chapter.
'It takes me about a week.' Then the typist arrived and
produced this first draft – she stayed overnight, as the

61

chapters were often very long: Chapter 4 ran to forty-two pages – maybe too long. Then the boys would come down for the weekend and the argument began.

'They use words I don't like.' He chuckled. 'Alan is very dogged and persistent. But he knows that when I say "no" that is it.' I replied that it was *his* book, so he couldn't have words put in that were not his style.

We are now on the Roman Empire and its decline, he explained. He had taken out the section called 'Great Captains' completely to save duplication and about 4,000 words. One week-end he had sat down and written 'Afterthoughts on Generalship', and was going to redraft Chapter 25. He reckoned the team was turning out about a chapter a month. Would I, on each diagram of a battle, put an arrow to indicate the nearest large town. Zama, for instance. We needed an arrow which said 'Carthage – 20 miles' – that sort of thing. I agreed.

Monty had removed the Battle of Britain from the list of battles needing diagrams and had substituted Crécy for Poitiers.

'I'll tell you why. I know the country. I've fought over it. You see, Edward III landed near Cherbourg and marched through Normandy. I know the whole thing, so I can make comments.'

I was delighted to hear him say this, because I had all along been pressing him to comment. I suggested that some battles required more than one diagram – phase one and phase two, for instance. He took to this idea. Then he said that in about a year's time he wanted me to come and stay for a couple of days and read the whole text from A to Z for sweep, balance, style and repetitions. Meantime, if I disagreed strongly with anything in the chapters and wished to make comments of any kind, he'd be delighted.

As he wanted me less than anticipated at the beginning, would I agree to my honorarium being reduced a little? 'What I suggest is that I take £500 off. When I thought I was going to use you terrifically, I said, "A thousand's no good. Make it two." Now I'll reduce it to £1,500.'

I said this seemed fair, as it appeared to involve less work. I am not sure it did so in the long run, and probably Monty got my services on the cheap anyway, but I was so interested in the project, that I would almost have done the work for nothing! Monty appeared to feel some embarrassment at this change, for he repeated his explanation that he needed me when he was alone, that we had done the first chapter and the last six together – 'a great thing for the boys to have: it put them right', because when they began work they were rather at sea. But once they got into the book they proved to be jolly good, and were really earning their keep. Monty told me that he had put pressure on George Rainbird to pay them an adequate salary. Obviously he drove them hard, and expected them to be working whenever he rang, even at ten o'clock at night.

Rainbird was going round Europe, selling the book to publishers in Finland, Spain and elsewhere. He was off to the Frankfurt Book Fair later in the month, taking the first three chapters and other bits with him. I enquired whether Monty was being paid a royalty on each copy sold. No, he was being hired as an author. 'He finishes with me the moment the book is handed in.'

The Field-Marshal admitted that he had learnt an awful lot of history. 'I didn't know anything about the early Greeks.' Not much more about the Roman Republic, I gathered. I too had already learnt a great deal. Were the boys producing the material in the form in which he required it? Yes, the themes came in sequence, and then he wove them into a story.

Monty had changed his mind and decided not to go to South Africa this winter. Instead he would stay in Bournemouth to get the sea air, and the boys would come down for three week-ends and discuss progress and the current chapters. They visited Isington once a month to go through the first draft.

'They mention some frightful name,' said Monty, 'and I say: "Where is this damned place? Nobody knows!" I quote the *Encyclopedia Britannica* at them. They say: "That isn't right." And I say: "I don't care what you say. This is the *Encyclopedia* and I go by that."'

He laughed, adding twice the words 'very funny.' Often Monty's laugh was a two-syllable 'huh huh!'

The title of the book had now been settled as *A History of Warfare* by Montgomery for *Montgomery on War* was too reminiscent of Clausewitz' work. For the colour jacket he would have the painting of himself – wearing beret and fleece-lined jacket against a map of Europe, though he'd be pointing, not at Normandy, but at another part, maybe the battlefield of Waterloo.

We then talked about his forthcoming visit to Sandhurst on 1st November to talk to the seniors. How many would that be? About 250: the cadets who would be 'passing out' just before Christmas. Monty thought he had better wear uniform for the occasion. What did I think they would want him to talk about? He never knew till the moment arrived, and then he talked extempore. The thing was not to be too serious. 'You've got to decide what you think is right, and then stick to it. It will get you into trouble. It got me into

Montgomery with Eisenhower at Gabès, March 1943

Montgomery in retirement at Isington

quite a bit of trouble, but I've emerged!' He laughed. That was the sort of thing he ought to say. Tell them what they're in for – what they're in for. About twenty minutes. After that the cadets would probably go to sleep.

What seemed to interest Monty most was the contrast between the present day and when he was a young man.

'The idea that Lord Roberts,* who was Commander-in-Chief of the British Army, should come and talk to the cadets – one never heard of such a thing. When I was a student at the Staff College in 1920, the idea that Douglas Haig would come and talk was unbelievable. We didn't even have the CIGS.' The present generation were lucky. The change was admirable.

I recall that on this occasion Monty said:

'Working with these boys is awfully good for me. It keeps me young.'

As usual he came out with me to the car, and walked through the gates to the road, to guide me out in case anyone came rushing down the hill.

Monday, 1st November 1965
Field-Marshal Montgomery spoke to the senior division of officer cadets in the Woolwich Hall at Sandhurst. Wearing his blue uniform and a larger spread of medal ribbons than almost anyone there had ever seen – ten rows – he looked a thin figure, less sunburnt than I had seen him recently, and a

* Field-Marshal the Earl Roberts of Kandahar (1832-1914) won a Victoria Cross during the Indian Mutiny. He commanded British forces in the South African War in 1900, and in the next year became Commander-in-Chief of the British Army until the post was abolished in 1904.

trifle wan. He was welcomed by the Commandant, John Mogg.*

'It's not easy for me to talk to you. We are such very different ages. I don't suppose there's anyone in this room who was born when I was here as a cadet. Would that be right? [*Laughter*]. You and I, we belong to the profession of arms, and in that profession it is going to fall to you to exercise leadership in some degree or other, some more and some less. Now don't think that because you leave here not having received promotion, or not having been thought good – it's too early to tell whether you will rise to great rank or whether you will slowly peter out. Now I, in my own case, I left here under a cloud, a very big cloud. [*Laughter*]. I was reduced to the ranks: I didn't mind that very much [*laughter*], I was put back a term – that I *did* mind – put back a term, and told when I left here that I was useless. My company commander – *he* told me. [*Loud laughter*]. It didn't work out that way. [*Laughter*]. The chap who was useless was really my company commander. He remained a major all his life [*laughter*] and I did not. So you never know!

'If you want to succeed in our profession, the profession of arms, there are a lot of things necessary, but I think two are vital. The first is that you've got to master your profession, and that means giving up a lot. But if you don't know your stuff you can't really go very far, nor will the soldiers follow you. They want to know that you really do know your stuff. And that means a great deal of really hard work. It means a great study of military history, deciding how the great

* Major-Gen. (later General Sir John) H. J. Mogg (1913-   ) was Commandant of RMA Sandhurst 1963-66. He afterwards served as Adjutant-General.

captains of past days did their stuff, when the conditions were quite different, and then equating it with the conditions of today.

'Now the second point is this: our profession is a great study of human nature. You see, generals are meant to win battles. That's what they're meant for. What you've got to understand is that battles are won primarily in the hearts of men. That's where they're won. Those are the two big things: master your profession, and understand the great problem is handling men – and women too. Much harder! [*Laughter*].

'Now I would like to give you three points which may help you at your level, which will be a pretty low level of animal when you start in. Three points. They all have to do with this thing called leadership.

'The first type of leadership would be leadership by authority. You may have a stripe on your arm, or be an under-officer. You may be a second-lieutenant. You have some authority. But that authority, by itself, means next to nothing. It merely gives you the opportunity to exercise a degree of leadership. That's all. And don't think that because you have authority you are necessarily a great leader.

'Now the second type is leadership by popularity. That is to say, you may be popular with your fellows. You're probably popular because you have rather more pocket money than they have, or you may have a fund of rather amusing stories and people gather round you. That's no good. It's a very empty form. The moment your money begins to dry up a bit, or your fund of stories dries up, these people will go away and leave you. It's a very empty form of leadership.

'The third form is what I would call leadership by character. That is to say that those below you know they can absolutely trust you, that you'll never let them down, that you have at heart their best interests. You will always be quite frank with them, and they will trust you and give you their confidence for these reasons. Now that is the right sort, and if you have authority, which gives you the opportunity, and if you have this character, then I would say that you are well set and great achievements become possible.

'Now the British soldier – I know quite a bit about him – the British soldier is a very easy person to lead provided you understand that he wants to know what is going on. In the 1914-18 War I don't think the soldier had the slightest idea what the thing was all about. That won't do today. I learnt pretty early on, and particularly in the late war – Hitler's War – when I began to rise to high command, that the soldier wants to know what's going on, what it's all about, and what you want him to do, and why you want him to do it, and when. If you do that with the British soldier, he will do anything for you. He will undergo great hardships, great privations, frightful discomfort in battle, the almost certainty of wounds and the probability of death. He will do the whole thing if you treat him properly and understand this human problem. That's how I see it.'

VII

As I could not get away from Sandhurst until after tea, I drove over to Isington Mill at six to discuss my comments on the abridged version of Chapter 4, 'The Ancient Greeks', and on Chapter 6, 'The Roman Defensive and the Barbarian Migrations.' I stayed to supper.

Monty was wearing a blue pullover, a dark brown shirt, a blue tie with a gold badge on it, navy blue trousers and brown shoes. He looked thin but well, his eyes were bright, and he had a good colour in his cheeks. 'I don't want to get a paunchy figure,' he said.

He mentioned several politicians. Of Harold Macmillan he observed: 'I wouldn't go into the jungle with him. If only one person was going to come out, it wouldn't be me.' He regarded Alec Douglas-Home as 'the perfect gentleman,' and he liked Jim Callaghan, who always gave him a naval salute. Quentin Hogg he would back to win the general election.

Monty talked about Sir Brian Horrocks,* for whom he obviously felt affection. He said he had brought Horrocks up from being an instructor at the Staff College, through

* Lieut-General Sir Brian Horrocks (1895-   ) commanded XIII Corps in North Africa and XXX Corps in North-West Europe.

commanding the Middlesex Regiment under him in France in 1940, and then as XXX Corps commander in the Eighth Army in North Africa.

'Anyone else would have died,' said Monty, referring to the severe wounds Horrocks had suffered.

At one point during 1944 Horrocks reported to Monty that he was not satisfied with his Chief Signal Officer and wanted another. So Monty discussed the matter with the Signal Officer in Chief and GHQ and was told by him: '— is the man for the post.' Monty informed his military secretary, who was to arrange the posting of the new CSO to XXX Corps. Then a message arrived from Horrocks to the effect that he would not accept the new man. Monty instructed his military secretary to tell Horrocks that this CSO had been appointed by Montgomery, the Army Group Commander. Still Horrocks refused, and said he would resign.

Next Monty telephoned General Dempsey, who commanded the Second Army, under whose direct control Horrocks came. Dempsey did not wish to get involved: it was, he said, 'a technical matter.' So Monty wrote a note to Horrocks telling him, as he put it, 'Not to be a bloody fool.' He then paid a visit to XXX Corps and said to Horrocks: 'We seem to have been having rather a hoo-ha about this Signals appointment.' He made Horrocks take the new man.

Later Monty reminisced about the funeral of Marshal de Lattre de Tassigny* which he had attended in Paris in 1952.

---

* Jean de Lattre de Tassigny died on 11th January 1952. Montgomery and Eisenhower, with an admiral, eleven generals and two NCOs accompanied the coffin from Notre Dame to Les Invalides. Montgomery and Eisenhower walked behind the gun-carriage, to left and right respectively, the one wearing a beret, the other in peaked cap.

On de Lattre he remarked:

'He could not divorce himself from being French.' When he went to Indo-China he was still C-in-C of troops in Central Europe, and he left a Chief of Staff there – an impossible situation.

As the funeral procession and service was going to be a lengthy affair, some of the older men were worried about their bladders and the lack of opportunity to pee. He himself felt dehydrated. Eisenhower, for the procession through the streets of Paris, required a special bag suspended inside his trousers.

*

The first Christmas card I received that year was Monty's, by at least a month. His cards were often more unusual, more particular to himself, than anyone else's I knew. For one thing they arrived so early: in four successive years the cards were posted on 9th, 1st, 12th and 4th November – even those for delivery within the United Kingdom. The 1965 card displayed two photographs. On the left Churchill, stick in hand, cigar in mouth, wearing a chain through his waistcoat button holes, leans on Monty's right arm. The captions reads:

'I lunch with my greatest friend Sir Winston Churchill, at his London home on 1st July 1964, and after lunch we go together to the Houses of Parliament.'

The right-hand photograph shows a pensive Monty, bareheaded, a white scarf round his neck, his hands in the pockets of his British 'warm' overcoat, looking down at a gravestone on which is carved WINSTON SPENCER CHURCHILL 1874-1965. Underneath are printed the words:

71

'He died on 24th January 1965 when I was travelling overseas. I visit his grave at Bladon* on my return – 31st May 1965.'

This, I suspect, reflected Monty's defence of his remaining in South Africa at the time of the State funeral in St Paul's Cathedral at which he had been invited to be a pall bearer – a conspicuous absence for which he had been criticised in the press.

Two years later his Christmas card again provided two photographs of Monty, this time in the war cemetery at Alamein. On the left he stands in uniform, hands clasped in front, against a background of gravestones. The right-hand photograph shows him in front of a memorial which bears the inscription:

THEIR NAME LIVETH

FOR EVERMORE

His hands, as before, are clasped, right inside left, with his right thumb on top of the left hand. In both photographs Monty's far-away expression under the peaked cap is profoundly sad. His eyes, at once sad and smouldering fierce, look sunken and ringed with fatigue. Normally he did not look at all pouchy, however pinched his face might be. The expression is like that when Monty was photographed wearing an Australian bush hat in 1942.

The Christmas cards for 1966 and 1968 both show Monty carrying the Sword of State. The first occasion was when the Queen opened Parliament on 21st April 1966, after the General Election. Monty holds the scabbarded sword in front of him, point upwards.

'I carry the Sword of State' reads an addendum to the

* Near Blenheim Palace and Woodstock in Oxfordshire.

72

description of the occasion.

On the second card, a colour photograph records the ceremony on 31st October 1967, when the Queen read the speech from the Throne at the opening of the Second Session of the Forty-fourth Parliament of the United Kingdom of Great Britain and Northern Ireland.

'This was the first occasion on which Her Majesty was accompanied to the Opening of Parliament by the Prince of Wales and the Princess Anne.'

Below, and printed in larger type, are the words:

'I carry the Sword of State.'

Monty's left hand grips the sword three inches above the hilt, and his right hand holds it a little higher.

*

On 11th January 1966 Monty went off to Bournemouth to get some sea air and was soon joined by Alan and Anthony. On the 20th, he wrote from the Carlton Hotel, East Cliff, to thank me for my notes and comments on Chapter 7: 'The Norman Conquests and the Crusades.'

His letter continued:

I know Palestine very well indeed, also Trans-Jordan, Syria and Asia Minor. I commanded the troops in Palestine in 1931, and in 1938/39 was Military Governor of northern Palestine when we were at war with the Arabs. I have visited the sites of many of the Crusader Castles and can confirm what you say about intervisibility – being visible to the next. I am inserting a sentence in the text on Page 24 to that effect.* I had forgotten about it until you

---

* See p.176 of *A History of Warfare*.

mentioned it. It is curious how one's memory of over 30 years ago can be awakened; and of course the most interesting part of the book may well be one's own personal comments.

I return home to Isington Mill on Sunday afternoon next, January 23.

From month to month, chapter to chapter, I begged Monty to comment more freely from his own experience and to add his own thoughts on war. His letter from Bournemouth had been in reply to my request that he should expand the bald statement: 'In 1931 when on garrison duty in Palestine I paid several visits to Mt. Carmel and surveyed the battlefield of Megiddo.' Such a comment shed no light. Nor did a reference to Marshal Zhukov as 'a good soldier whom I know well.' Surely he could have provided so much more than: 'In the gap between the Jura and the Vosges, very well known to me . . . .'

There was scope for personal observations when Monty referred to Pitt 'not allowing Wolfe's advance to be blocked by resentful and more senior officers' or wrote about Wolfe's 'early years of striving and preparation to fit himself for the opportunity whenever it might come.' Had not Monty himself done precisely this?

Instead of quoting someone else on life in the Western Front trenches, why not give his own description? Could he not draw comparisons between the hurried planning of the Gallipoli landings in 1915 and the prolonged preparations, based on the lessons of the Dieppe raid and the invasion of Sicily, for D-Day? Now and then I felt the Field-Marshal had been too harsh in criticising a commander for neglect and error, or else had over-simplified the circumstances in which

74

a man had made decisions.

Another category of comments I offered dealt with repetitions and contradictions, statements requiring an illustrative example, paragraphs which struck me as too staccato in style, and sentences where the order of words could be rearranged with advantage. To avoid an excess of dates I proposed alternatives like 'in the following year' and 'ten years later'. Obscure places were mentioned in the narrative without any indication of where they were. In more than one chapter I argued in favour of 'British' rather than 'English' when writing of troops, expeditions, strategy or shipping.

For the early chapters I either wrote or typed my comments page by page, line by line, and posted them to Isington. But by November 1965 Monty had rightly decided that this was a laborious method. 'Would it not be simpler,' he wrote, 'if you brought your copy here one evening and we sat together and I entered your comments in my copy?'

So it came about that I drove to the Mill and discussed all my comments over tea. Frequently I failed to persuade Monty to accept a suggested change or interpolation. He would sit in one corner of the sofa, pen in hand, typescript laid out in front of him, and he would ponder each point. He made up his mind quickly and either adopted a point and entered the amendment in red ink, or else he brushed it aside and waited to deal with the next.

Sometimes I used to watch Monty on the sofa and wonder how this small spare man, with his air of calm, his alert look, his incisive way of speaking, his vulnerability, his courtesy, had been able to command up to two million troops, Most men held jobs which had their own special expertise, yet were within reach of other human beings. But to command an army and an army group in war, to have such colossal responsibilities in terms of life and death, of ultimate victory or dreadful failure seemed almost superhuman. His now mellowed personality had dominated men and events. He had made tremendous decisions and not changed his mind under pressure. His pen which now altered a typescript had signed documents of infinitely greater importance. Those eyes which were usually kind and benevolent had often flashed with contempt and anger . . occasionally I had to work my imagination hard to see in the relaxed Monty I knew the uncompromising, harsh, yet inspiring general of twenty years before.

Wednesday, 2nd March 1966
Michael Cox, the plump, red-faced chauffeur-cum-gardener, came in to collect the mail.

'There, on the shelf,' said Monty, pointing to a small pile of hand-addressed envelopes. 'Don't put them in your pocket!' he added with a twinkle.

When I left, Monty saw me off and came out to my car. 'Everything's coming out,' he commented, waving at the roses and other plants.

He did not bother with an overcoat, and walked across the drive to the double gates. He looked outside at the road, signed to me to wait while a car went past. Then he stepped right outside and waved me forward. I turned right and up the hill to Bentley and home.

Monday, 23rd May 1966
I parked my car in the drive at Isington Mill, usually outside the front door facing towards the gates so that I shouldn't

keep Monty waiting by laborious turning of the car if he came out to see me off the premises, as he often did. He had long since told me I need not ring the door bell: I could walk straight in and up the stairs to his sitting-room. As usual he was on the sofa, reading, this time Lord Birkenhead's review of Lord Moran's *Winston Churchill: The Struggle for Survival*. Monty looked up and launched straight in. 'Ah! How are you? Have you read this?'

I had bought the book that very morning in Camberley, having read extracts which had been appearing in *The Sunday Times*. Monty had demanded a copy as he was mentioned in it and wanted to see what Moran had said. He disliked the idea of quoting what someone had said about another person, though he admitted that Moran was a good writer. Monty had known Moran 'terribly well – terribly well', even before the war. I enquired how he had become Churchill's doctor. Monty said *he* had a doctor too: Bob Hunter.*

'The army appointed a doctor to look after *me*. I never bothered him, never even had a cold, but he was there, watching me. I think once or twice he said: "You're looking rather tired." And I said: "Well, this war's going on a long time."' He chuckled.

I told Monty he was rather like Wellington in this respect. He was the only one of his senior generals who never went home ill from the Peninsula, because, fortunately for Britain, he never had anything wrong except an occasional touch of lumbago. Wellington was only forty-six at Waterloo. How old had he, Montgomery, been at Alamein?

---

* Robert B. Hunter, afterwards Professor of Pharmacology and Therapeutics at the Universities of St Andrews and of Dundee, and from 1968 Vice-Chancellor and Principal of the University of Birmingham.

'I was fifty-five, and fifty-seven in Normandy. Oh! it's a big difference.'

He had been drinking tea and at this point realized that I had not. 'Get another cup. Ring that bell.'

He began telling me about a visit from Alan Clark, who was writing an introduction to a reissue of Alan Moorehead's book *Montgomery*, to coincide with his eightieth birthday. When the housekeeper came into the room, Monty said to her: 'We want another cup.' Then he went on about Alan Clark's book *The Donkeys* about the generals of the First World War and which he had just read – a frightful story and largely accurate. It was clear to him that the generals of the period had no doctrine of command. He knew Rawlinson* and several others and wouldn't have had them near him.

The only decent one, in his opinion, was Smith-Dorrien† whom he had visited in St Malo just before he went to the Staff College as a teacher early in 1926. Monty had been in his corps at Le Cateau. Probably he was the only general who realized the frightful things that were going on and refused to accept them.

'They sacked him. Dreadful, absolutely dreadful!'

Monty laughed, whether out of disgust or glee or some other feeling I could not say. Often one could not interpret the tone of his dry laugh or chuckle.

He brought the conversation back to Lord Moran and press reaction to his book, and the family's protests, and

* Sir Henry Rawlinson (1834-1925), later Baron Rawlinson of Trent, was given command of the new Fourth Army in France in 1915.

† General Sir Horace Smith-Dorrien (1858-1930) commanded the 2nd Corps at Le Cateau in August 1914 and during the subsequent retreat. In December he took command of the Second Army but disagreed with Sir John French and retired.

Moran's need for money to settle on his children in a trust. Monty had read the book in bed, all 800 pages, and it was too long. He, too, had known Churchill since 1940. He told me he had a book in his own hand-writing, locked away in the safe. It was really an album of photographs he took himself of the old man when he was terribly ill, in 1963. Taken in bed.

'From 1960 onwards I practically lived at Chartwell. It's called *My Association with Winston Churchill*, but I wouldn't *dream* of publishing it.'

I suggested that he owed it to posterity to put down on paper his recollections of Churchill. He said he had done so, beginning with the conversation at their first meeting after Dunkirk* when Monty had said: 'I don't see how on earth we can win this war,' to which Churchill had replied: 'Nor do I.'

Monty went on to say that, having spent a whole day on the south coast, he had declared: 'Now we shall win because we've got the man. A man of great decision and courage. But *how* we shall win I just don't see at the moment.'

That was one of the extraordinary things about the British at war. Somehow we held on to the belief that somehow, sometime, we would win. It had been like this at the beginning of August 1942 when I reached the Alamein Line on the same day as Monty assumed command of the Eighth Army. After the ordeals and disasters of June, the savaging of our tanks, the virtual destruction of whole infantry brigades, the grievous fall of Tobruk, after the costly struggles during July to make a defence line and to hold the triumphant enemy there, and after the vain efforts to force him to retreat in his turn, morale might well have been very

* Churchill spent 2nd July 1940 visiting Montgomery's 3rd Division in the area of Brighton.

low Perhaps it was low at Army Headquarters, where staff officers were drawing up plans for a withdrawal to the Sudan, just in case of need, and were talking in despondent tones. But in the 5th Indian Division which I joined as a very inexperienced subaltern things were different.

As I listened to the recent memories bubbling out over basic food and drink or in quiet interludes at work, I began to envy my companions. They had the tired euphoria of survivors. They had emerged from the frights and the battles and the 'gold rush' of a retreat. Now they relaxed and took new heart. In the telling their stories veered from the tragic to the wildly funny and exciting. Close to the front I found everyone more casual and more easy-going in certain respects than had been the case in training and reinforcement camps round Cairo. There we had been ordered to attend classes laden with steel helmet, water-bottle, gas-mask, emergency rations, pistol and ammunition, just as if German paratroops were expected to land at any moment in the courtyard or on the sand. Perhaps they were; and the precautions were wise. But up the Desert people said: 'What in Heaven's name are you humping all that clobber about for?'

It seemed to me that, although ignorance was in no way bliss, the more a man knew about the war, the more difficult he must have found it to retain his faith in ultimate victory, even in a single theatre of war. I suspected that morale declined the higher you went. Consequently morale at battalion and brigade headquarters was liable to be better and more resilient than at corps and army. Since the end of 1940 the desert campaign had been like a military see-saw, with first one side and then the other advancing to the limit of its supply lines, only to be driven back part of or all the way by an enemy who was like a coiled spring, with supplies close at hand. Hope and disappointment had taken turns to predominate. Success had never been total and definitive, so it had seemed vulnerable and transitory. So had failure and setbacks. If there was always another chance, then it could be seized.

Army Headquarters was of course the first to be influenced by the arrival of a new general in the person of Montgomery. In five weeks his impact had not filtered down very far by the time my division was pulled out of the line. It was the defeat of Rommel at Alam Halfa that heartened the troops, though General Montgomery's order of the day told us that 'the Battle of Alamein has now lasted for six days and the enemy has been slowly and surely driven from Eighth Army's area.' No mention at the time of Alam Halfa.

Much has been made of the low state of morale at the time of Montgomery's arrival. Churchill had described the men as 'brave but baffled'. It was the deliberately unexploited success at Alam Halfa as August made way for September, plus the sight of fresh divisions from Britain and superior American tanks, which really pumped up morale to the very high pitch required by Montgomery for the twelve-day slogging match of Alamein.

Next we turned to my battle plans of Breitenfeld and, page by page, went through my comments on Chapter 12, 'European War in the 17th century.' He told me he'd been having a row with George Rainbird and William Collins over the number of pictures and diagrams. On this number depended the number of copies Collins would take of the book, a difference between 50,000 and 35,000.

Had I seen a letter written to *The Sunday Times* by a boy from Manchester in response to Monty's article on the battle of Hastings? No, but I had read the article. Monty had invited the boy to lunch with him at the House of Lords the following week, and had written him asking him to consider: What is the first rule of strategy? 'You won't find it in any book. I learned it by hard experience.'

Monty was obviously looking forward to hearing the boy's reply to his question, so I pressed him to say what was his own first rule.

'The commander-in-chief must be sure that what is strategically desirable is technically possible with the resources at his disposal.'

Some people had thought it was strategically desirable to go to Greece, but it wasn't possible, Administration was essential. 'You've got to be sure that what you want to achieve in front is commensurate with what you've got behind,'

Italy was a good example, in his view, of a campaign where the administration was never up to the growing operational commitments. Had I read his book *From Alamein to the Sangro*? He had made the point there. Monty had the disconcerting habit of suddenly asking people if they had read this or that of the books he had written. So often the reply had to be 'No'! Not that he appeared to mind, and in any case he often asked with a twinkle in the eye, or else the momentum of thoughts carried him on past his question.

On this occasion the mention of Italy led him to talk of how much Churchill liked Alexander:

'Alex always agreed with Winston. Winston rode roughshod over everybody, and everyone gave in until he met Alanbrooke. He didn't like him. And I would say "no". Alex never did, and he was Winston's blue-eyed boy.'

Surely, I pointed out, Churchill had liked Montgomery in spite of saying 'no'. After Alamein he had been on a good wicket. Monty corrected this to Alam Halfa, but I replied that not till after Alamein was it conclusively a good wicket. Monty repeated what I knew already, that Churchill had realized that if we lost the battle of Alamein he was out. Parliament wouldn't have stood for a defeat there.

He then talked about nineteenth century warfare, and the lack of large-scale British wars after the Crimea, and the red tunics worn by soldiers going off to war. He recalled being a small boy in Tasmania during the Boer War of 1899-1902. Seeing soldiers marching off was one of the things that made him be a soldier. 'We had a Tasmanian contingent. They must have had a battalion. I said: "By gum! That's the stuff!"'

In a letter dated 11th July 1966 Monty wrote:

Thanks for your comments and ideas for improving Chapter 12. I have catered for all your ideas, and have added many personal comments and illustrations of what I have said. Now we are coming to the more modern times I am well able to do this. For instance, I have reconnoitred the route of Marlborough's route to the Danube by air, and parts of it by car, and by steamer on the Rhine – and have said so.

VIII

Thursday, 29th September 1966

A propos of nothing in particular, Monty mentioned a battalion mutiny when they got back from Dunkirk. The battalion was in his 3rd Division.

'A frightful thing,' he remarked. 'I rang up the Major-General and said: "I'm not touching this. You come and do it." They were under my command, but it was very delicate. So he came down and removed the CO. Out!'

I cannot say I liked the hard voice, the dismissive style, in which Monty said the word 'out', and the way in which, now and again, he told such stories. Although in retirement he had mellowed tremendously, one occasionally heard echoes of the harsh bark and the ruthless cut which had earned him such dislike in certain quarters and which, after the war, had caused to circulate so many stories in which the Field-Marshal appeared in a hostile light.

That same day he told me another sacking story. Churchill, he said, wrote a paper in 1941 which included the phrase 'Renown awaits the general who will first mass his guns.' The paper became known in the Army as 'Renown awaits'.

Monty chuckled at this title, then added, very characteristically: 'I was the first to do it. Renown awaits!' He laughed again.*

Did I know that he had sacked his head gunner? I certainly did not. While preparing for Alamein, and even earlier when the battle of Alam Halfa was on, he noted that the head gunner of the Eighth Army liked to give all his guns away, to 'scatter the Desert with little troops of cannon', as he phrased it. This would not do at all for the next set-piece battle, so Monty sent for the senior gunner at GHQ Middle East and said:

'Martin† must go. He can't do this. For Alamein I want artillery of a thousand guns, like a battery.'

The senior gunner replied: 'Martin? A delightful person. He was amateur golf-champion of Ireland.'

To which Monty retorted: 'This isn't golf.' He sent for Brigadier Sidney Kirkman** to replace Martin.

In fairness to Monty he enjoyed telling of occasions when he himself was almost sacked. He certainly laughed even

---

* This refers to a note, dated 7th October 1941, and circulated by Churchill as the Minister of Defence to various high commanders. The opening sentence runs: 'Renown awaits the Commander who first in this war restores Artillery to its prime importance upon the battlefield, from which it has been ousted by heavily armoured tanks.' For the complete text, see Churchill's *The Second World War*, volume III, *The Grand Alliance*, pp 442-44.

   Monty did not see this paper until Churchill showed it to him in Tripoli in 1943. Renown by then certainly attended his restoration of artillery to its place upon the battlefield.

† Lieut.-Gen. H. G. Martin, who retired in 1942 and became military correspondent of *The Daily Telegraph*.

** Later General Sir Sidney Kirkman, who became Quarter-Master General to the Forces 1947-49. In 1942 he was Brigadier Royal Artillery of the Eighth Army.

more, in the knowledge that he came out from the episode unscathed, even with advantage. For example, in 1940 he set up a brothel in Lille for the men in his division, under the doctors' supervision, as one way of reducing the incidence of venereal disease. There was a frightful row.

'The padres got hold of it and Gort wanted to sack me.' He laughed gaily, perkily. Alan Brooke, the corps commander, said to Gort, 'No, leave it to me. I'll handle him. You can't sack my best general.'

Gort consented, and Monty was ticked off by Brooke. He chuckled again as he remarked: 'A ticking off by Alan Brooke was quite something, I can tell you!'

Monty then asked whether I knew that Tedder had published his war memoirs*. Cassells, he said, had delayed printing them for two years and *The Sunday Times* had refused to serialize them. I enquired why this was so. Were they libellous? Monty told me that the book slanged the Army, the Navy, everybody except the Air Force. *The Sunday Times* asked: 'Will you review it?' Monty replied: 'Certainly.'

'And I've reviewed it,' he said. 'Tedder won't like it. I've shot it absolutely down in flames.' Apparently Tedder wrote in his preface that he did not believe in official histories. Monty believed very much in them. As far as he was concerned, it was the record of events that counted.

In his review Monty quoted the fact that Tedder told Eisenhower to sack him. Did I know that? Tedder, said Monty, had been unwise enough to send a copy of the letter to

---

* *With Prejudice* by Marshal of the RAF Lord Tedder. Monty's reply to some of Tedder's sniping and denigration appeared in *The Sunday Times* dated 9th October 1966, and complemented a review of the book by Michael Howard.

the Air Ministry. This was done on 23rd July 1944. Two days later the Allies broke out from the Normandy bridgehead. Monty laughed.

Tedder, he remarked, had never liked him since the Desert days, when after Alamein the Eighth Army got up to the Jebel, beyond Mechili. He then sent Monty a signal telling him what he should do next. So Monty said to Freddy de Guingand: 'You can tell Tedder that I'm capable myself of handling the land battle. I don't want any advice from the back area in Cairo.' Monty had written this in his review. From that moment on, Tedder had hated him. Or so Monty claimed.

'I've said it's odd that this man, one of the very great airmen, which he was – one of the great airmen – should write thus about the Army. It really shows a warped mentality.' He chuckled at this, and then asked me whether the words 'a warped mentality' were libellous. If they were, he had instructed *The Sunday Times* to change them. I said it probably depended on the whole tenor of the review. The words were certainly hostile, but maybe not technically libellous.

That afternoon we went through Chapters 14, 15 and 16. These dealt with Frederick the Great, Napoleon and Wellington, and the Mongols, Chinese and Japanese. We discussed the use of the terms 'British' and 'English', and in many cases he altered 'English' to read 'British'. I persuaded him to change his first reference to the onslaught of Napoleon's cancer to read 'dysuria', or retention of the urine, from which he suffered at Borodino. He felt that readers could look up the word 'dysuria', so he omitted the reference to urine. I had checked in several books and had come to the conclusion that Monty could well be shot down if he mentioned cancer at this stage of Napoleon's career.

I raised objections to his reference to Wellington before the Waterloo campaign opened. Monty appeared to assume that Wellington knew where Napoleon was going to strike, and to overlook Wellington's fears for his line of communication to Ostend. Even during the battle he had kept 17,000 troops out by Mons and Hal to guard against this threat.

'You can't get away from that,' said Monty, quite sharply. 'He was dancing. I can't imagine myself doing that!'

Nor could I, either professionally or socially, but I explained that Wellington had gone to the ball to show a bold front and to keep up morale. Monty pressed the point that Napoleon had been allowed to place his army between the British and Prussian forces. I told him that Wellington had admitted that he'd been humbugged and caught napping, but Blücher's message about the opening French moves had taken a frightful time to reach Brussels.

I said I felt the Field-Marshal would agree that if a commander has made all his plans, as Wellington had done by midnight on 15th June, then he could go to sleep, or go to the ball. He had done his work. His staff and commanders could carry on. Had not Monty himself during the battle of Alamein given orders that he was not to be woken unless a real crisis blew up?

Monty changed the subject by relating that he had recently been to the Old Bailey, where Quentin Hogg had been pleading a defence in court. He had been asked to sit opposite Hogg at lunch.

'Quentin's a good friend of mine. Do you know Quentin?'

Again I did not. Again Monty was notching up another old friend. He said to Hogg: 'Quentin, our party has no leader. Heath is totally undignified. Totally. The way he goes on, calling people asses. You can tell him from me, he's undignified.'

When Hogg queried this, Monty replied: 'Certainly. From me.' This made him laugh. He then defined politics as 'a struggle for power by ambitious men.' He had already said this once in the House of Lords, he declared.

The next friend he mentioned was once again Liddell Hart, whom he got to know as an education officer up in the Potteries. 'Sometimes he was very critical of me. Now he thinks I'm not too bad!' He laughed. He said that when L.H. was military correspondent of *The Times* and *Telegraph* he was considered 'a great guy'. How Monty cracked out these words! Of all the historians he put him in front of A. J. P. Taylor, whose *Origins of the Second World War* he thought extremely good, even if Taylor did overstate his case now and then.

Liddell Hart, ten years younger than Monty, had recently had the same operation for prostate gland. He got trouble while in America and wrote to Monty from Los Angeles to say he was returning home at once. Could a bed be fixed for him in Sister Agnes'? Monty wrote immediately to Miss Saxby, the matron there, and then to Badenoch*, who had performed the operation on him:

'Get ready to do Liddell Hart.'

By this time L.H. had been knighted. Monty claimed that he had persuaded Basil to accept the Knighthood. Should he not be given the Order of Merit? 'They wouldn't give the Order of Merit to a journalist,' Monty declared, rather contradicting what he had said about Liddell Hart as an

---

* A.W. Badenoch, the eminent urologist.

historian. Anyway, Liddell Hart had cabled from America to Number 10, Downing Street, accepting a Knighthood.

I said how glad I was, because everyone had felt he should be honoured.

'Of course,' said Monty. 'They call him "Master".'

He had said: 'Now look, Basil, you've got to be extremely careful for six months. Do nothing. But he wasn't, and had to go back into hospital.'

This remark was unfair on Liddell Hart, who was more seriously ill than Monty had been.

On this occasion he told me he had been asked to write an article entitled 'Montgomery versus Rommel'. He would have to decide whether Rommel could be classed among the great captains, and this was very difficult. He could have been, was Monty's conclusion, but Rommel had served a very unpleasant political master. Moreover, you cannot be placed among the great captains unless you have won campaigns against really good generalship. Rommel didn't. Here Monty returned to a well-worn theme of his:

'In the Desert they couldn't touch him. No one could compete with him. They weren't any good.'

I suggested that Rommel was never knocked out decisively before Alamein. Monty conceded that he had retreated several times, but he had been obliged to do so for administrative reasons. But he never fought really good generals. Had I known Ritchie,* Godwin-Austen† and all

---

* General Sir Neil Ritchie (1897-1984), Deputy Chief of Staff Middle East, 1942; commanded Eighth Army 1941-1942; commanded XII Corps 1944-45.

† General Sir Alfred Godwin-Austen (1889-1963) commanded XIII Corps in the Western Desert 1941-42 and then asked to be relieved of his command. After holding two War Office posts, he became Quartermaster General in India.

the others? 'The best general was O'Connor.* Captured!
Neame†. Useless!'

O'Connor had not been given sufficient credit for his
campaign:

'Do you know Dickie? Gweat friend of mine.'

For once I could say 'yes'. He had visited Sandhurst on
two occasions to talk to members of the Napier Society, of
which I had been secretary, and I had dined with O'Connor
at Peter Young's house beforehand. I refrained from telling
Monty that so many cadets had remarked 'What a modest
man!' O'Connor certainly made a distinct contrast to Monty.

I was shown the draft of the article, and we had quite an
argument over one phrase Monty had used, when he stated
that Rommel 'didn't pay sufficient attention to' administration. Phrases like: 'I have got to attack, and if the stuff doesn't
come by Tuesday, we shall have to go without it.'

Monty reiterated that one of the planks of his own strategy
had been to ensure that the stuff behind was commensurate
with what he wanted to do in front. 'Otherwise I won't do it. I
wouldn't attack at Alamein. I refused to.'

How would I word the sentence? I suggested 'Rommel
could not ensure . . .' With the best will in the world he
could not because he was let down by insufficient effort on the
German-Italian side and too much effort by the RAF and
Navy. How about 'He was not in a position to ensure . . .?'

---

* General Sir Richard O'Connor (1889-1981), Military Governor of
Jerusalem 1938-39, commanded Western Desert Corps against the
Italians 1940-41; was captured; escaped from an Italian camp 1943; he
commanded a corps in France 1944; was Adjutant-General 1946-47.

† Lieut.-General Sir Philip Neame VC (1888-1978) commanded the
4th Indian Div. Western Desert 1940; GOC-in-C and Military
Governor, Cyrenaica, 1941; captured 1941; escaped from Italy 1943.

Montgomery had certainly taken advantage of his enemy's lack of resources, but to call it a 'weak point' in Rommel's conduct of war implied that he did not really grasp the need for administration. Surely the only alternative would have been for Rommel to retreat.

Monty admitted that in Rommel's position he would have said: 'I'm going back. I'd never have asked. I would have gone back to the frontier and the wire. Maddalena and Halfaya. That would have made things very awkward. It would have shortened his L. of C. And lengthened mine.'

I asked whether Monty had drawn up any plans in case Rommel had pulled back.

'I knew he wouldn't,' came his instant reply.

Had he really taken a safe gamble, because of Hitler's orders?

'Yes,' Monty chuckled.

Surely, if Rommel had retreated, all our pipelines and other things would have been left in the middle of the desert. Monty said that after passing Mersa Matruh we should have got away from the Sweet Water Canal and been obliged to bore for water. He still considered his original sentence could stand. I still demurred. Was it unfair? Oversimplified, possibly. I should have preferred 'could not ensure'. Eventually Monty proposed a slightly verbose compromise version which ran: 'Rommel was unfortunate that he could not pay sufficient attention to ensuring that . . .' We settled on that formula. I never saw the finished article in print.

Before leaving Isington Mill that afternoon I asked Monty whether he would sign my copy of *Forward to Victory*, which contained facsimiles of all the personal messages he had issued to the Eighth Army and 21st Army Group. He did so in red ink, with the black pen he had been using earlier to correct the typescript. He always made corrections and changes in red ink. He hoped I didn't mind if he used it for the inscription, and he apologised for putting the wrong date — 30 instead of 29-9-66. He drew my attention to the first message dated 23-10-42: 'The battle which is now about to begin will be one of the decisive battles of history.'

'I don't think even Napoleon said he was going to fight a decisive battle . . .' Monty began.

'Not in advance,' I put in.

'I did,' said Monty with a smile.

On 4th January, 1967 Monty wrote from Isington and sent me the draft typescript of Chapter 19.

It is short, only 20 pages and a bit. I have decided that a battle plan of TSUSHIMA is *not* needed. We have now started work on chapter 20, the 1914/18 War. A battle diagram will be needed from you of TANNENBERG.

This chapter 19 comes to you early. I got it finished during the Christmas period!

On Saturday next, January 7, I am going with the research team to the sea at Bournemouth; we are all feeling a bit jaded! So send me there the battle diagram of Gravelotte, and any further comments you have on chapter 18. Address: Carlton Hotel, East Overcliff, Bournemouth.

Tel: Bournemouth 22011.

I return here on January 22.

Thursday, 26th January, 1967

On his homecoming Monty asked me to telephone him to

agree a date when I could go over to Isington to discuss Chapter 19 and also to tell him about my three weeks' visit to Rhodesia. I had stayed in Salisbury with an army friend from Burma days and his wife.

'I would very much like to hear about your experiences,' he had written. 'I have always reckoned that the whole affair has been grossly mismanaged by the British Government.' I had been in Rhodesia a year after UDI.

In another letter dated 17th January 1967 he wrote:

We are going to face a terrific problem with Chapters 20 and 21 – to write a clear story of a world war in one chapter, which most authors give a book to, or several volumes! If I haven't gone mad by 1st May, I shall be surprised; I hand in the completed typescript to Rainbird on that date. I then go off to the Alamein battlefields on 4 May.

So here I was, talking in the sitting-room at Isington Mill, just as before. I noticed the thin blue veins on the back of Monty's hands. He wore a blue and red striped tie, a brown shirt, and his usual blue sweater and blue trousers. For an hour we worked on Chapter 19, 'Learning the Hard Way', which deals with, *inter alia*, the lessons learnt from the Crimean War, the American Civil War, the Franco-Prussian War and the Russo-Japanese War. Points of detail, amended dates and initials, small insertions, deletion of sentences which belonged properly to the next chapter dealing with the Great War, avoidance of repetition of the same word in a sentence and of *non sequiturs*.

I suggested here a cross-reference, there a stylistic improvement, now a change of tense, now a clarification to help the reader. We argued about phrases or paragraphs where I had pencilled in 'Why?' or 'Where?' or 'What nationality?' Monty himself had already corrected in red ink most of the typing errors – barely a dozen in twenty foolscap pages.

When we had finished our work and had either agreed on changes or agreed to differ, tea was brought in. Monty's invitation to eat sandwiches prompted me to ask him what he had eaten in the Desert.

Bully beef. Dehydrated vegetables. Very healthy! Tea. Every day boiled eggs. The Arabs, he recalled, used to call: 'Eggis! Eggis! Eggis!'

He mentioned the Sweet Water Canal and remembered one occasion when he had to move the whole of Eighth Army because the water contained curious salts which gave the soldiers diarrhoea.

I said I had met men who had campaigned up and down the Desert and claimed they could recognise the source of water merely by its taste – Mersa Matruh water, for example. Monty said they were often on very short rations of water: a man would be on half a gallon a day.

This was sometimes true, although my recollection of the Alamein Line during August 1942 was that the normal water ration extended to one gallon a head per day for all purposes. Despite having our faces, arms and knees coated with sand whenever we drove across the desert or the wind blew up, we could never take a bath and had to get used to washing seldom and skimpily. Some planned to wash a third of the body each day, but to do even this required skill if one was also to shave, clean one's teeth and wash one's feet – all in one mug of water.

After use for washing in the early daylight, the water would be left until the evening wash, and might even be kept overnight and used again before the glutinous liquid, thick with soap, dirt, stubble and toothpaste, was poured through a strainer into the radiator of a jeep or truck. Occasionally I managed to wash socks and pants. Less successful was my first attempt to wash the sand out of my hair: I used too much shampoo, worked up an excessive lather, and then had nothing like enough water for rinsing my soapy hair!

Monty also told me that his troops used to barter tea leaves, and got very clever at this. 'They would keep the tea leaves out of the pot after they had been used several times and give them to the Arabs.'

Did the Arabs realize this? Of course not.

'Rather naughty!' I said.

Monty laughed, adding that once the Arabs did realize what the soldiers were up to, they became much more skilful in their bargaining.

Monty declared that *A History of Warfare* would be his last book. 'One's getting a bit old for this game.' He told me that he had just had to renew the licence for a ·22 rifle because Michael had shot a starling. The licence, 'for vermin destruction at Isington Mill,' had cost him half a crown.

He was obviously delighted by a recent incident. As he was driving along a road he noticed a red-haired primary schoolboy thumbing a lift. He stopped the car and said: 'Hop in!'

Then he asked: 'Do you know who I am?'

The boy had no idea.

'I'll give you a clue. I'm a field-marshal.'

'Oh, good! I want a job working in the fields myself. Do you drive a tractor?'

'No, I kill people.'

Isington Mill

Isington Mill showing the hangar where the campaign caravans were housed

The boy looked startled. 'Stop the car, please. I think I'll get out.'

Friday, 17th February 1967

I took morning coffee in the upstairs officers' mess at Sandhurst. I was talking to a group of friends when I felt a tap on the shoulder and turned to see an officer whom I barely knew.

'Field-Marshal Montgomery is waiting to see you in the entrance hall,' he said.

My first reaction was that he must be pulling my leg. Had it been from someone I knew well, this might have been the case. However, I quickly realized that this officer meant what he said, so I left my coffee cup and hurried downstairs. There stood Monty, bareheaded, wearing a dark blue duffel coat. Fortunately he was not waiting alone, thanks to a colonel who had known him years before in Egypt and had introduced himself. They were deep in conversation.

Monty had been driven over from Isington so as to hand me the typescript of Chapter 20, 'The 1914-1918 War,' on which he wanted my comments in a hurry.

We were discussing this when I noticed my colleague David Chandler walking towards me. Seeing me talking to a duffel-coated figure, David jumped to the wrong conclusion that this was a lecturer from another department who was nearing retirement age and who did, in fact, bear some resemblance to Monty. Under this misapprehension David felt he could break into our conversation and pass me an urgent message.

As he did so he must have seen me giving him a peculiar look. Up to this point he had paid no attention to my companion. Suddenly he did so and realized who it was.

Words dried on his lips. For a moment his mouth gaped in appalled astonishment, but he quickly recovered his aplomb.

'Who's this?' Monty asked.

Hurriedly I made the introduction.

'What does he do?' said the Field-Marshal.

'He's just published a major work on the campaigns of Napoleon.'

'Any good?'

'Yes, sir, it is.'

On hearing this, Monty turned to David. 'I hope you gave Wellington what for.'

Then he stated his well-known belief that the first rule of war was:

'Do not march on Moscow.'

I told Monty that David Chandler was also an authority on the campaigns of the first Duke of Marlborough.

'Well Chandler, you know that Marlborough and Montgomery have the M the right way up. Wellington – an M upside down. No good at all!'

Monty said this in a jocular manner and laughed.

Of course he assessed Wellington much more properly than this. On 1st October 1969 he sent me a typescript to which was pinned a handwritten note which read: 'Since you have written a good deal about Wellington, you may care to have this copy of the Memorial Lecture I gave at the R.U.S.I.'

In this lecture Monty had conceded that Wellington was a master of the conduct of war, that what made him 'tick' was his intense sense of duty, that of all the military commanders who emerged from the Napoleonic campaigns he alone took his place among European statesmen. But he faulted the Duke for not possessing the quality of inner conviction which enabled a great commander to 'throw his bonnet over the moon'.

'One cannot too much admire his foresight, industry, patience and meticulous care,' said the Field-Marshal of Wellington. 'Yet he sometimes lost part of the fruits of victory through an inability to soar from the known to seize the unknown. Napoleon never surpassed Wellington's flawless handling of his command at Salamanca and Vittoria. But the defeated French after Vittoria would never have escaped to fight another day had Napoleon been in command of the British army – or maybe Cromwell!'

Monty was not on firm ground in making this particular criticism, for had not the Afrika Korps and Italian forces under Rommel's command escaped after their defeat at Alamein at Monty's hands and fought another day, at Mareth above all?

Reverting to 17th February 1967: Monty had written a letter to accompany Chapter 20 – the 1914-1918 War – which he had decided to bring by hand so that I should have it before the weekend. In it he wrote:

It has been difficult to deal with it in a single chapter, but it has been done, and I am well satisfied with it. It needs a battle plan of Tannenberg. It would be a great convenience if you can send me any comments you may have on Chapter 20 as early as possible – and the battle plan of Tannenberg. These last two chapters (20 and 21) are so difficult to write that we have been forced to put the programme back a bit. The last chapter (21) will not be typed and ready for you until Friday March 24, Good Friday. Where will you be on that day? Does the R.M.A. disperse for Easter or remain in session? I could bring it to you by car that day. There will be no posts over Easter. You will want to see it before you come here on Friday March 31 for the weekend.

Chapter 21 will need two battle plans: Midway 1942 (sea battle), Meiktila 1945.

Then he had added in scarlet ink: 'Please telephone me today: any time after 12.30 p.m.'

This letter typified Monty's meticulous and thoughtful planning, his attention to detail, and his consideration of other people who helped him. So too did the notes about Chapter 21 which he sent with the typescript:

Under the heading *Alamein, page 23*:

Draft a sentence saying why I have dealt shortly with Alamein. It will not be disputed that I on one side and Rommel on the other were the decisive figures in the Battle of Alamein. I would have liked to discuss the battle with him. But he is dead, and we cannot tell the story together. I have written a great deal about it in other books, but in this 'history' I feel that it is enough if I place the conflict in its right place in the historical canvas.

In the end he merely wrote that for reasons of space he had written briefly about Alamein. I had earlier persuaded him to deal with Slim's masterstroke at Meiktila which provoked the fiercest Japanese reaction but strangled their defence of Mandalay and the Irrawaddy River.

Next, under *Infantry, Page 33*, he wrote:

Draft a sentence, or two, which can precede what I have written, or follow it, pointing out how the role of the infantry soldier has changed over the ages – together with his weapons and tactics. In fact, I have written a great deal about this in Chapter 20, which could be referred to.

He also agreed to write more about Churchill. This he did, though not in the personal terms which I had proposed.

Monday, 27th February 1967
Monty quoted the soldier who had described the Desert as 'miles and miles of absolutely damn all,' and said: 'He was just about right.' He wanted to revisit the battlefield of Alamein for the twenty-fifth anniversary. He related how, on arrival in Egypt in August 1942 to take command of the Eighth Army, he had found the Headquarters right inland and a long way from the Royal Air Force, who were by the sea. He pointed to a map: 'It seemed to me that the Army and Air Force were rather inclined to fight two separate battles. My whole concept of war was that if you fight on land it must be an army-air battle.' So he moved Eighth Army HQ beside that of the RAF at Burg el Arab, half way between Alamein and Alexandria.

After he had been there a few days Winston Churchill paid a visit. They had not met since 1940. He wanted to see how Monty was getting along. 'He wanted to find out, to see me in action.' Monty turned out of his caravan to make way for the Prime Minister and took himself off to another caravan.

Monty added that after a long day spent in visiting units one arrived back very hot and covered with dust. 'I remember one evening very well. Winston said: "I want to bathe." I said: "Certainly." And he advanced on the beach down here in a shirt, blowing in the wind.' This took place on 19th August.

IX

As early as January 1966 Monty had told me that he would ask me to spend a weekend at Isington to read the whole typescript for 'balance and sweep.' So I was not surprised to receive a brief note from Isington Mill, signed merely 'M of A'. It read as follows:

> When you arrive here on Friday drive your car into the right-hand garage — which will be open. You need not close it; the gardeners will do that before they go off duty at 4.30 pm. Don't bring a lot of clothes. I wear old clothes, and never change in the evenings — being alone, and buried in the country.

Friday, 31st March 1967
I reached Isington at four o'clock and parked my Rover in the right-hand garage: both parts of this had been built into the house and were under Monty's bedroom and dressing-room. Michael Cox appeared immediately. I had often seen him before when he came to the sitting-room to collect letters for the post or to fill up the stove with fuel. When Monty gave up driving, Michael took over.

Now he began to close the garage doors even before I had

climbed out of the car. Then he took my bag and led me past a signed photograph of Marshal of the Soviet Union Konstanstin Rokossovsky* – had he been relegated to the garage? – and into the ground-floor dining-room. I walked upstairs, left my bag on the landing, knocked on the half-open door and went into Monty's room.

He was dressed in a navy blue polo-necked fisherman's jersey, navy blue trousers and black shoes. First he took me up one flight to the second floor, where Alan and Anthony worked at weekends whenever they came down from London. He led me through into the bedroom, told me which of the two beds had been made up, and opened a wall cupboard to reveal a washbasin. He explained how the hot water switch worked, and also opened the hanging cupboard for my clothes – I had brought very few.

He went downstairs again, telling me to join him for tea when I was ready. Later he took me up to what was to be my workroom and offered a choice of two desks. Alan Howarth used one of them, and this I chose as being the larger and better placed for the window light. I was shown a drawer full of foolscap paper; indeed, the desk contained nothing but office equipment, paper clips, erasers and the like. It had been presented to him on 7th July 1947, by the Devonport, Hobart and Launceston branches of the Royal Society of St George, at Launceston in Tasmania.

* Marshal of the Soviet Union K. Rokossovsky (1896-1968) began the Second World War in command of a mechanized corps, but soon rose to be commander of an army and then of several fronts. His troops took part in the destruction of the German forces at Stalingrad, in the Battle of Kursk and in many operations all the way to the Elbe in 1945 via Warsaw and East Prussia. Rokossovsky, described by Monty as 'an imposing figure, tall, very good-looking, and well-dressed', first met the Field-Marshal on 7th May 1945 at Wismar.

A light russet-fawn carpet lay on the floor, which, like the doors and bookcase, were of Tasmanian oak; while under the corner desk a reddish rug bore in its centre the crest of The Royal Warwickshire Regiment 6th Foot worked in blue, grey and white. On this desk stood a wooden pen tray carved with a crest and presented in August 1958 by HMS *Alamein*. Between the two bedroom doors a small table, covered by a claret cloth, held various framed photographs – some taken by Monty himself, with an excellent lens – of his grandchildren Henry and Arabella and his godson, Jeremy Soames: by a tree at Chartwell, at Eton, and elsewhere.

The window sill at the garden end of the room was adorned by a toby jug of Monty wearing his beret. Over the mantelpiece hung a mediocre watercolour by James Greig of St Brelade in Jersey, while on the mantelpiece itself stood Monty's armorial bearing, with his motto '*Gardez bien*', in colour and framed. On a central table the last three or four issues of *Punch, Country Life* and the *Illustrated London News* were carefully laid out, so as to overlap – not unlike a permanently tidy officers' mess anteroom or a consultant's waiting room. For comfort there were two white armchairs, but I never had time to sit in them! Indeed, except for meals and an occasional short walk in the garden, I spent most of the next fifty hours in that top-floor flat, either working under pressure or else sleeping from sheer exhaustion.

On the landing outside my room hung a bare-headed portrait of Napoleon, a signed photograph of Margot Fonteyn in ballet pose, dated 1947, and a drawing by Maurice Adams of the Church of St Gervais in Falaise. Right at the top of the stairs was an oil portrait of Montgomery by a South African war artist named Neville Lewis. Monty said many people considered it the best portrait of him: it is certainly an excellent likeness, and again shows him wearing the familiar beret*.

The other two large portraits in the house were by James Gunn and Frank Salisbury. The former hung in the dining-room, in a row of family portraits – from right to left, Monty's great-grandfather, grandfather, father, himself by Gunn, and his son David. Gunn stayed at Monty's headquarters in France and painted him in beret, light blue sweater, seated rather stiffly erect in a sideshelter of his caravan.

Frank Salisbury's portrait hangs in the study. It shows the Field-Marshal, wearing beret and fleece-lined jerkin over his beribboned battledress, and standing against a map of Europe at which he is pointing, with his right hand to the base of the Cotentin peninsula. In May 1945 Salisbury stayed for two weeks at headquarters, which were on Lüneburg Heath. He was already an old man, and for the first week he just sat about, watching Monty and making a few sketches. Then he painted the portrait in two long days, working ten hours a day. Afterwards he went to bed and rested. Monty contrasted Salisbury's method of absorbing himself in his subject with Gunn's method. Of the latter Monty felt that he was painting a duchess on Monday, a Lord Mayor on Tuesday, and so on – always a different sitter.

In 1932 Salisbury had painted Monty's father, the bishop, in mitre and golden robes, about a month before his death at the age of eighty-five. At lunch one day Monty looked at this

---

* Neville Lewis (1895-   ), RP, served in the First World War, painted native life in South Africa and portraits in Spain, the USA and England. He was an official war artist with the South African Forces, 1940-43, and painted Churchill, Smuts and Alexander as well as Montgomery.

portrait in the row and observed: 'You can see how frail he's looking.'

At tea Monty talked about the timber built into his converted millhouse. After the war it was virtually impossible to obtain hardwood in Britain. All the timber for the floors, doors, cupboards, book-shelves etc. was of Tasmanian or Victorian oak, given to him by the Australian Government who also provided the caravan barn in the garden. The wood used in his study was Australian cedar. The Canadian Government gave the cedar shingles for the roof.

'The only government that gave me nothing was my own!' he remarked tartly.

On the Friday and Saturday afternoons we had tea in his study as usual. The Dutch cook had made a very good iced orange cake. Monty had none of it, but he did eat several homemade 'biscuits'; and on the Sunday when I was working against the clock and he kindly carried tea on a tray up to my room, he took a piece of an excellent and rich chocolate cake – to encourage the cook who, at her own request, was known as 'Ree', though this was not her name.

Meals were always served very punctually in the ground-floor dining-room at Isington: breakfast at 8.30 (nine o'clock on Sunday), lunch at 1.00, dinner at 7.30. The Swiss maid sounded the gong very long and loud – unnecessarily so in my opinion, but Monty explained at least three times during the weekend how this custom had started when 'the boys', as he always called them, had said they could not hear the gong when immersed in work on the top floor. Now he was reluctant to change the instructions, in case the maid went and sounded the gong too quietly!

Monty was always ready at mealtimes, not least for

breakfast. On the sideboard, laid with a white cloth, stood the coffee pot, with milk keeping hot in a thermos jug. Beside it was a plate of butter cubes. For me two boiled eggs were served, each in its cup with cosy, and done just as I like them, nearly firm, though I had said nothing about my likes in this matter. Monty ate very little – he kept on telling me this; but he liked coffee, and drank it four times a day. Toast, butter and marmalade: we each had a small silver toast-rack holding four thin triangles with the crust cut off.

At other meals Monty would ring a little hand-bell when we were ready for the next course. The Swiss maid carried in dishes on a tray, all excellently cooked: for example, we had chicken fricassée, muslin potatoes and spinach. Another day we enjoyed very good thin steaks. At one lunch she produced a first-rate apple-pie – I am something of a connoisseur in apple-pies, a favourite dish. I helped myself to what I considered a large slice, but Monty insisted at once that I cut a second slice. 'We shall never see it again once it leaves here!', he said, implying that the staff might eat whatever remained of the food they served.

Monty said that his main meal was lunch and, as I knew already, he ate very little in the evenings, but he never stinted me. On the Friday evening he asked which wine I would like to drink: Claret, Liebfraumilch or Riesling (he pronounced it Reisling). I chose the Liebfraumilch. He admitted he knew nothing about wines, but he enquired the date on the bottle (1962) and whether it was all right. It was, and it lasted me well for two evening meals and one lunch. Monty drank water. We helped ourselves to cheese and biscuits and then poured out coffee from the sideboard: a bowl of pink and white coffee sugar stayed on the dining table.

So, too, did a bowl of small oranges, in the centre, where I sat facing the row of family portraits. Monty sat at the left hand end of the table, while at the opposite end were a bowl of bananas and another of Cox's orange pippins. He always encouraged me to take another apple. 'Take two,' he would urge with a twinkle. He usually ate one himself, but he insisted on getting up and selecting one, and would not allow me to pass a bowl down to his end of the table.

During Sunday lunch Monty, wearing his pale blue sweater and fawn cord trousers, noticed that the white handkerchief he pulled from his pocket had a tear along the border. He turned the handkerchief round till he found the name tape: 'M of A' in scarlet. This, he explained, indicated that it was an old one, because the current name tapes read 'Montgomery of Alamein' in sloping scarlet letters.

On the Friday evening after supper I sat upstairs working through the chapters, one by one, and was on the point of stopping when Monty came up to riddle the Esse Autovectic stove, beside which stood two hods of fuel. He had gone to bed at half past nine to read, and now appeared in a claret coloured silk dressing-gown, below which showed his blue and white pyjama legs.

'Still struggling?' he asked in a friendly way.

He told me that this stove and the one in his study used about five tons each during a winter, at £18 a ton. Michael riddled them at midday, and he did it himself in the evening.

Next morning I woke early and could not get to sleep again, so I rose at six, shaved and had a bath – alas! a tepid one, for, as Monty explained later, the hot water was not turned on as early as that. Wearing my blue sweater and sports jacket I sat working for two hours before breakfast, and the room was beautifully warm. The landing door was left open at night so as to allow the heat to circulate.

When the maid came in at 7.15 to draw the curtains she was astonished to find me writing at the desk. On the Sunday morning I woke even earlier, partly because I had many chapters still to read and comment on. Again I got up and this time did three hours' work before breakfast. I felt hungry, so when the maid came in I asked if she could bring me a glass of cold milk, an apple and a banana. She did so. When I addressed her in German I found that she came from Bern, and spoke Swiss-German better than *Hochdeutsch*. She said she missed the mountains and the snow. She was good enough to compliment me on my German. At breakfast Monty approved when I told him of our conversation. He approved even more of my early start to the day's work!

Needing a short break during the Saturday morning I took advantage of the sunshine to wander round the garden, especially on the hill above the house and over the stream, and having asked Monty's permission, I took a dozen photographs, including a few from the windows of my flat. The Field-Marshal, meanwhile, had been driven off to Lloyds Bank in Farnham to draw out money with which to pay his staff on the Monday. He also drew his old age pension from the Post Office: not every week, but once in three or four weeks. Otherwise, he explained, if you let it go for longer than thirteen weeks, you had to go through a complicated procedure to draw the pension in arrears. On his return he told me he had been to Holy Communion, which he did whenever Sunday was to be a working day on the book, as, for instance, when the boys came down for the weekend. The congregation, he remarked, consisted almost exclusively of women.

Throughout my stay at Isington I found the constant rushing sound of the millstream very soothing. I was conscious of the noise most of the time, but no doubt those who lived in the house became accustomed, even oblivious to it. All Sunday pouring rain added to the sound. After breakfast Monty said we needed some gentle rain for the garden, but by the afternoon he was admitting that the rain was a good deal harder than 'gentle'.

At one point I asked him where he first started the system of having liaison officers. North-west Europe, he said. In the desert he had relied on two extra ADCs. The liaison officers all lived in 'B' Mess at Headquarters, and had to go wherever he sent them. Every night they had to be back and mark up his maps. They had to have finished their meal by nine o'clock and be ready outside the map office.

'One by one they came in. Winston loved sitting there listening to them. So did the King. Loved it.'

Each one in turn would report where he had been that day, what the situation was at the front, and what the generals thought about it. As a result Monty knew far more about the war than did Eisenhower, who saw the ordinary operational sitrep which went off from Main Headquarters. Monty would, after the liaison officers had given their reports, sit down and write a secret telegram to Alanbrooke.

I enquired whether he told the LOs where to go and what he wanted them to find out. Monty would say: 'I don't like what's going on up there, and I want you four to get up in that area. I'm very anxious to know what's going on.'

Was there ever any sense that they were snooping? I asked. None at all. 'The point about the boys was that they had to be awfully nice lads who would be welcomed by any general.'

He admitted that sometimes it could be a tricky business, because the LOs would by-pass Army HQ, but they would call in at Corps, where they were well known, and let the staff know they were in the area and proposed to visit this or that division. They would do this and say to the general, or to his GI if he was out:

'The Commander-in-Chief has sent me down to see you. He is very anxious to know what is happening on the front of your brigades.'

According to Monty the general concerned would be frightfully pleased; and when the liaison officer reached brigade headquarters and said 'The Commander-in-Chief has sent me to see you', the brigadier, said Monty with a chuckle, 'thought he was going to be immediately promoted!'

What happened, I asked, if the LO reported that General X said this, that and the other, but that in his view the situation wasn't nearly as rosy as the general had pictured it? Monty would keep this under his hat amd make some non-committal comment such as: 'Oh! Very interesting.'

The work was very dangerous sometimes, especially once the whole of 21st Army Group was across the Rhine and driving forward on divisional axis, by-passing the Germans. To be quite safe you had to travel up a divisional axis, but occasionally the liaison officers would cut across country instead of driving up one axis and back down the next.

'It was a very tricky business,' said Monty, 'and three of them were killed.'

I asked how he picked the liaison officers in the first place. Did he ask somebody on his staff to produce one for interview?

'They were personally selected by me – *personally* selected.'

The first three had been with him in the desert and he knew them well. When he wanted more liaison officers he would say: 'Now, do you know any really good chap?' Maybe someone who had been at school with them. Once Monty had a possible name he would go and see the officer without him being told the reason, and by the time Normandy came along he had built up a team.*

'It was,' he claimed, 'an entirely new system of operating command, except I suppose that Wellington had generals.'

I assured Monty that for Waterloo Wellington had eight ADCs and liaison officers.

Monty told me how one evening he gave instructions for all his liaison officers to wait behind. When the last had finished giving his report, they all came into the map room, rather apprehensive and wondering why they had been summoned in this unusual manner.

Monty addressed them. 'You lads have done me very well. I'm going to give each of you the Military Cross (he pronounced it 'crorse') – *each* of you.' Then he pinned the ribbon on each man's uniform. He explained to me that he had power to do this without War Office approval. He kept the ribbons in large boxes. Of course only the Sovereign could bestow such decorations, but he had said to the King:

'You must remember, sir. If I give someone the DCM or MM, the lift to morale is terrific. He can immediately wear the ribbon. He might be killed next day.'

---

* The liaison officers in April 1945 included: Major John Poston, 11th Hussars, who was killed in Germany in the last week of the war; Major T.E.B. Howarth, the King's (Liverpool) Regiment, who was later High Master of St Paul's School; Major J.R.E. Harden, DSO, MC, Royal Tank Regiment, who was elected Ulster Unionist MP for Co. Armagh in 1948; Major Charles Sweeny, Ulster Rifles, who was also killed in Germany at the end of the war in a road accident; Major Peter Earle, who was wounded; Major John Sharpe, MC (and bar) RA, afterwards General Sir John Sharpe; and two United States Army officers, Majors Brisk and Frary.

So the King allowed it. If Monty wished to award a Military Medal, for example, Private X would be sent for from the front line. Monty would pin the ribbon on his chest and send him back to the front. Monty said he could even award a DSO. His Military Secretary merely sent in a list: 'The Commander-in-Chief had made the following awards . . .'

This conversation led me to ask whose idea it had been that the troops who actually fought at Alamein on 23rd October should be allowed to wear an '8' on their Africa Star ribbon.

'That was the Cabinet – Winston.'

I said that it would have been much fairer to mark a man's presence at this turning-point battle by letting him wear a small 'A' for Alamein. The present decision had aroused so much resentment.

Monty agreed. It was, he claimed, Winston who laid it down. He himself had written about the matter, but to no avail. He had taken it up again after the war when he was CIGS, but had failed. He admitted that it had created enormous resentment and still does. 'Even the day *before* the battle – no. Alam Halfa – no.'

Perplexity, resentment, even indignation simmered for many years after the war. When I came to write a history of the 5th Indian Division with which I served for three years, one senior general said he hoped I was going to put in some strong comments about the 'scandal' of the Africa Star. I did not do so, but I understood his feelings and those of a great many other veterans of the Desert War. A man could have served with the Eighth Army for eighteen months and still not be entitled to wear an '8' on his ribbon. Nor were three commanders of the Eighth Army, and of its predecessor, Western Desert Force: Sir Richard O'Connor, Sir Alan

Cunningham, Sir Neil Ritchie; and, of course, Field-Marshal Sir Claude Auchinleck, who, while Commander-in-Chief Middle East, had twice taken over personal command of the Army in a desperate hour and restored its position and its confidence.

No doubt the decision was made as a means of distinguishing the prestigious Eighth Army from the British First Army, which landed at the far end of North Africa under American command and whose members affixed a '1' to the ribbon of their Africa Stars. To wear the ribbon unadorned could also be regarded as a distinction of a different kind.

During one meal Monty talked about the First World War and related how, as a subaltern, he carried a sword as well as a pistol. On the first day of mobilisation all officers' swords had gone to the armourer to be sharpened.

'I went off to war with a sharp sword. I drew it. At Le Cateau I charged the Gemans.'* The next time he drew his sword was at the First Battle of Ypres, where his battalion, the 1st Royal Warwickshires, had to attack on two sides of a road. No other orders had been issued except that they were to attack. Monty chuckled.

'I drew my sword and rushed forward towards the Germans. I hadn't the slightest idea where the Germans were, actually, but it was quite safe to go east. My God! We rushed forward and captured the village. My platoon was the only one to get into the village.'† He added that he had been badly wounded and awarded the DSO.

---

* On 24th August 1914.

† This occurred in the village of Meteren, south-west of Ypres towards Hazebrouck, on 13th October 1914.

Did he, I asked, ever carry a weapon during the Second World War. Yes, he always carried a .38 revolver. What about a personal escort – a man with a tommy-gun trailing round with him? Only in Palestine before the war. In Hitler's war he was never in front of his own lines.

From Normandy to the Baltic, wherever he went, he had two police jeeps, one in front, and one behind. 'Even when I was driving about in Normandy, one never knew.'

Talk of weapons reminded him of how he had discovered one of his pistols at Isington and thought he ought to hand it in, but as it needed cleaning first he decided to ask the Parachute Regiment, of which he was Colonel, to do this for him. So he rang up the Aldershot military exchange and said: 'Put me through to the depot of the Parachute Regiment. The *depot*.' He was put through to the adjutant, who picked up the receiver. 'Adjutant speaking.'

'This is Field-Marshal Montgomery here.'

'Oh! Get off the line, you bloody fool. I've had you before, saying you're this chap and that. Get off the line!'

Monty said: 'Would you mind if I spoke to your colonel?'

An appalled silence fell. Apparently the adjutant was talking to the telephone girl who told him:

'I would be careful, sir. This call *is* coming from the Field-Marshal's house.'

After a very awkward silence the adjutant came back on the line and said: 'I'm terribly sorry, sir, but I was hoaxed the other day. A fellow officer rang up and said: "The Duke of Edinburgh speaking.' "

Monty was very amused. 'Don't worry,' he said. 'Come and see me.'

He took a liking to the officer, told him what he wanted, and the revolver was taken away and cleaned. While

115

lunching soon afterwards with the officers of the Parachute Regiment, Monty told this story, the officer concerned being in the room at the time.

'You have the great distinction of being the only regiment in the British Army in which a captain has called a field-marshal a bloody fool on the telephone!'

During Sunday lunch he pointed to a colour photo of himself in Garter robes, and asked me if I knew why his page had red heels to his shoes. And why was Monty wearing the sash of the *Bath*? I had no answer to either question. He replied to the second that he was already wearing the collar and jewel of the Garter, so had no need to wear the sash as well, and could wear that of the next senior order, the Bath. As for the red heels, I never discovered why.

Monty related how one little boy had written to ask for his autograph. 'I thought you were dead, but my father tells me you are not, so will you please send me your autograph.'

This had so amused Monty that he had obliged.

Unknown to me, Monty had instructed Michael Cox to clean my car on the Saturday. 'A service I give to all my guests,' he said brightly.

He told me that Anthony Wainwright's car, which stood out in a London Street, was often frightfully dirty.

'I don't know what yours was like when it arrived, but it looks brand new now.'

In fact, my Rover had been fairly clean, but on weekdays it often stood outside, and was anything but new.

Michael, wearing his best Sunday suit, as Monty had forecast, arrived back just as I was packing up to leave. Otherwise Monty and I would have had to open the garage doors and the gates leading on to the road. These were kept shut and locked except when someone was expected. Monty walked over to my car, patted the bonnet, asked the make, and approved. During one meal he had told me that he had no idea what went on under the bonnet of a car. He had never needed to know!

X

After this exhausting, pressurised weekend I would not see the Field-Marshal for at least two months. Sandhurst was about to break up for the Easter recess, and I was going on holiday to Vienna for the first time. Soon after my return Monty was due to pay his formal visit to Egypt, with the prime object of seeing the Alamein battlefield close on twenty-five years after his victorious battle there.

On 3rd May he flew to Cairo and stayed once again at the Mena House Hotel near the Great Pyramid. I had spent several weeks under canvas nearby in 1942, and with three fellow subalterns who were also learning Urdu had toiled up each of the Pyramid's four corners on four successive evenings. Now, in 1967, Monty, accompanied by Sir Oliver Leese, formerly Commander of XXX Corps in the Eighth Army, and by Brigadier Hugh Mainwaring, who had been taken prisoner during the pursuit after Alamein, saw his erstwhile seashore headquarters at Burg el Arab. With the aid of old campaign maps laid out on the sand, of his own recollections and those of his companions, many of the key points on the field of battle were found. Monty wore white trousers, tennis shoes and a long-sleeved blue shirt; Leese preferred khaki shorts and a white shirt; while

Mainwaring had dark trousers, a grey shirt and a trilby hat.

The Field-Marshal stood again on the ridges of Miteiriya and Ruweisat, where in August and early September I had served as a very inexperienced subaltern who was often hard pressed to find his bearings in a landscape almost bereft of landmarks. Monty and his party stayed in a new hotel close to Alamein and travelled from one point to another by four-wheel-drive vehicle unless it was more appropriate to clamber, with helping hand and push, into a helicopter, not least for crossing the minefields of long ago.

Wearing full-dress uniform Monty laid a wreath of poppies at the Commonwealth war cemetery which overlooks the battlefield. He approved the Egyptian War Museum and at a press conference he denounced Britain's actions at Suez in 1956 as morally wrong. Now honoured with a full-scale reception from senior Egyptian officers, now entertained to lunch by the Governor of Mersa Matruh, Monty carried out a packed programme, sparing neither himself nor those with him, notwithstanding the heat and his eightieth year.

In the remainder of the ten days' visit to Egypt, Monty had a private talk with President Nasser, lectured to Egyptian officers at the Nasser Higher Military Academy, and walked into All Saints' Cathedral in Cairo to see the memorial window to the Eighth Army.

He flew back to England on 13th May. Three weeks later Egypt and Israel were at war – the Six Day War, in which Syria and Jordan also brought their military strength against the state of Israel, and lost.

The next letter he wrote me was dated 13th July 1967:

Liddell Hart has been anxious to see some of the chapters of my book and wanted to lend a hand with reading the

119

galleys. I declined this offer, and have told Alan that he is not to show him any of the chapters – and please act in the same way if you are approached. He is a very great friend of mine. I have told him that I do not want him to see anything of the book until it is published, because I then want him to review it – saying that he has not seen it before. When he does see it, he will I think be astonished!

He is writing a history of Hitler's war in *one volume*.* He knows that we have done it in *one chapter*, and he wants to see how we did it!!

Thursday, 27th July 1967
Monty took the salute at the Sovereign's Parade at Sandhurst, and addressed the cadets after they had marched past in slow and quick time. In the course of this speech he returned to several themes dear to his heart.

'You and I are soldiers, and as officers our raw material is men. Men are human beings and their lives are precious, not to be risked in battle without good cause or risked when other means will serve. You have to learn to command and control men. You will never be able to do that satisfactorily until you first learn to command and control yourself. I was never told that when I was cadet here, nor was I told it at any time during my first years as a junior officer in the Army. I had to learn by hard experience. I *should* have been told. You are lucky. You cannot now say that you have *not* been told because *I* have told you!'

One of the company commanders at Sandhurst, Major J.D.F. Alexander, Royal Tank Regiment, whom I knew through playing cricket for the Sandhurst 'Wanderers', told

* *History of the Second War* by B.H. Liddell Hart (1970).

120

me how he had driven to Isington to fetch Monty for the parade.

Although he was already in full dress with medals, the Field-Marshal had not yet put on his Garter sash. He asked Alexander to do this for him, presumably as a way of putting the major at ease.

Two large black cars had been brought from Sandhurst, just in case one of them broke down. Monty was favourably impressed by this insurance cover, and asked to meet the two drivers. Fortunately Alexander had briefed himself and knew not only their names but something about them.

In the car he found that Monty never stayed long on any one topic of conversation. He mentioned his visit to Egypt and to the Alamein battlefield, and told Alexander how, on his return to England and just after the Arab-Israeli War broke out, the Queen sent for him and jokingly enquired whether he had started the War.

'No, ma'am. And if Your Majesty's Government had listened to what I told them, there would be no war now.'

Alexander tried to draw him on President Nasser, but they were just driving through Aldershot, and Monty interrupted to point out a signpost to MONTGOMERY LINES.

Now that the writing of *A History of Warfare* was finished, I ceased to have any regular correspondence and meetings with Monty. It was late January 1968 before I had occasion to write to enquire whether he could persuade George Rainbird to spare me a set of proofs of the book, because this would be very useful for teaching purposes, the foolscap typescript I had being very bulky. On his return from Bournemouth he explained that there *were* no proofs. He asked when I was going to drop in the for a cup of tea, so I telephoned to suggest Thursday, February 1st, since I was dining with friends near Farnham that evening. He looked in his diary, then said in his briskest tone: 'That's *après-demain*, isn't it?' I failed to grasp what he had said first time, so he repeated it. His pronunciation was in fact quite reasonable, but I simply wasn't expecting him to break into French! Anyway, he invited me to tea at half past four.

Thursday, 1st February 1968
As usual I let myself in and walked up to his sitting-room. The Field-Marshal wore a light blue jersey, cord slacks, and black slippers. Over tea he explained that he liked being a member of the Athenaeum because he met no soldiers there. This, he declared, was in sharp contrast to the 'Rag'*, where 'People you don't want to see come up and talk, while those you like don't venture to approach.'

In March he sent me a copy of *Hansard* which covered a recent debate on Defence in the House of Lords. On the front cover he had written in scarlet ink: 'My speech begins in Column 241.' Monty had expressed his sadness at the disappearance of the Durham Light Infantry, 'the regiment which marched with me from Alamein to Germany and never put a foot wrong.' I too had been very sad to see the regiment go, for I had good friends in it and, above all, my younger brother Ivor had been killed while leading a platoon of its 9th Battalion in Sicily twenty years before.

Monty had referred in his House of Lords speech to the second rule of war: 'Do not go fighting with land armies on the mainland of Asia;' and had reiterated his first rule: 'Do not march on Moscow.'

* The Army and Navy Club.

The copy of *Hansard* had been sent by Monty because he believed that the officers at Sandhurst to whom he had talked informally after attending an Alamein Company Dinner would be interested to read the full text of what he had said.

Now and then Monty would pass on to me books which had been sent to him and he did not want to keep, such as illustrated booklets on British armoured cars, German tanks and armoured vehicles, and a very good Canadian publication called *The Tools of War, 1939-45*.

Thursday, 23rd May 1968

Monty talked about the biography of him which Lord Chalfont had undertaken. At the start Chalfont and his wife, a children's doctor, had been several times to see Monty, who had told Chalfont he must discover what made him tick.

The last time Monty and the Liddell Harts had stayed together in Bournemouth, Kathleen* had told him she had been pondering the same question. She believed it was Monty's early struggles with his mother and his refusal to give in.

'She's probably right,' he said. 'It must have had an effect on me.'

Then he told me, not for the first time, how, when he was about nine, he was caught smoking. 'I only did it because I wasn't bloody well allowed to.' He was reported by a gardener or maybe by one of his brothers – he could not remember.

'We had in the house a small chapel. My mother wasn't available at the moment, so my father took me into the chapel

---

* In 1942 Liddell Hart married, as his second wife, Kathleen, daughter of Alan Sullivan of Toronto and widow of a surgeon named H.P. Nelson.

and we knelt down and he prayed for my forgiveness from this great sin I had committed. Silence. He prayed again. Another long silence. Then he said: 'My son, you have been forgiven.' I was beginning to feel rather good, but when we went outside, my mother was waiting for me, cane in hand, and I was beaten – not on the *derrière* but on the hand.'

I asked why his mother had been so rigid in her attitude. It was, he believed, because she had married when she was only sixteen.* His father had been one of Dr Farrar's curates at St Margaret's Westminster and when he began courting the daughter he would be told that Miss Maud was 'at her lessons'. She was indeed still at school. Anyway, she celebrated her 17th birthday while on honeymoon. They moved to St Mark's Kennington, a large parish, and children began to arrive. By the time his mother was twenty-five there were four boys and a girl. She was so busy with her duties as a parson's wife, and later as a bishop's, that her one rule was that 'we had to do as we were told or get beaten. My brothers were much more amenable than I was.'

Although he always talked a great deal about his own doings, Monty had a great and genuine curiosity in other people and was liable to ask question after question. Had I read any of John Masters' novels? He had disliked his latest. Did I know Fred Majdalany's book on Alamein? 'It's the best. He put the battle in a strategic setting. You can't deal with a battle in a vacuum.' What had I read at Cambridge? And what sort of degree had I got? Had I been to Durban? No, but I had spent three days on board ship in Cape Town harbour, in January 1942. Most of the large troop-carrying

* Henry Montgomery became engaged to Farrar's third daughter, when she was fourteen and he thirty-one. They were married two years later in July 1881 and spent their honeymoon in Donegal.

convoy from England had gone to Durban and thence to Singapore and captivity in Japanese camps. We had been fortunate in steaming up to Suez and the Middle East.

One day he referred to separate visits to Isington by two military historians. He liked them both, but commented with a laugh: 'All these chaps talk. They talk, talk, talk. It's extraordinary!'

In June 1967 he wrote to ask me for the name of the Commandant of the Regular Commissions Board at Westbury. He knew that I had been there once to watch what happened and to follow the fortunes of one small group of candidates during the interviews, discussions, and outdoor tests.

'I saw on TV on Friday night a film of the 'goings on' at the RCB, which interested me greatly, and I may go there to get a first-hand view – and have a look at the intake. If I *do* go, where does one stay?'

I told him, but do not believe he ever went.

XI

Early in September 1968 I spent a week on holiday in
Copenhagen. When acknowledging a post card I sent him,
Monty wrote:

> The Fredericksborg Castle is well known to me, and I
> have seen my coat of arms as a Knight of the Order of the
> Elephant several times. Alas! The insignia of the Order
> was removed by the burglars who ransacked my home in
> November last year, when I was in London for the night.*
> And the King, whom I know well, has not shown any
> gesture to replace it!
>
> The publication date of *A History of Warfare* is Monday
> September 30. It is a superb production by Rainbird. I
> told George to send advance copies to Alan, Anthony and
> to you – and I hope he has done so. Let me know if he has
> not.

* Monty had gone to the Royal Hospital Chelsea to a dinner party in
celebration of his eightieth brithday on 17th November 1967. Thieves
who broke in that night took gold, silver and jewellery, the star of the
Order of the Garter, his field-marshal's baton, and the insignia of the
rare and very valuable Order of the Elephant, presented to him by
King Christian X of Denmark. He was succeeded in 1947 by King
Frederick IX.

I would like to see you again and have a talk, if you can get over here one afternoon for a cup of tea. But telephone first to agree a date.

I arranged to drive to Isington for tea on 15th October.

My copy of the book duly arrived by post, on 24th September, and in the author's acknowledgements, after richly deserved praise of Alan and Anthony, and all the really hard work they had put in, 'day in, day out, with no holidays,' I was very pleased to read:

> Then I needed somebody who would be apart from the research team, but who would help me by reading the chapters as they were produced, and comment freely. I looked for an experienced military historian; his further task would then be to draw sketch plans as references for the diagrammatic battle plans we needed. I found exactly what I needed in Antony Brett-James, Lecturer in Military History at the R.M.A. Sandhurst, and himself an author of military works. His knowledge and help were invaluable.

Tuesday, 15th October 1968
I visited Monty for tea at Isington Mill. He was wearing a navy blue sweater, navy blue trousers, and black slippers. His eyes were strikingly blue, though a trifle bloodshot.

He had laid out on a table several reviews of the book, and expressed particular pleasure that it topped the non-fiction bestseller list. He inscribed my copy in generous terms.

During tea he told me how a certain Brigadier Gribbon*

---

* Colonel Walter Harold Gribbon (1881-1944) commanded the Canal Brigade in Egypt.

(King's Own) was in Khartoum when he himself was commanding the 1st Battalion of his regiment, the Royal Warwickshires, in Alexandria. Gribbon hated Monty because he was jealous of him. Moreover, I was told, he didn't know his stuff. Monty's was the best battalion in Egypt at the time: his own verdict of course. Yet Gribbon wrote a very bad annual confidential report 'which would have absolutely finished me if I hadn't been known at the War Office.'

Monty merely initialled the report as having seen it, but not necessarily agreeing with it. The report went up to the Commander-in-Chief, General Jock Burnett-Stuart.*

'Did you ever know him?' asked Monty, and then went on to say that Stuart wrote on the report: 'I don't agree. Lt-Colonel Montgomery is one of the best officers in his rank.' Then he sacked Gribbon.

'The dog it was that died,' I remarked.

On another occasion when Monty told me of this episode, he gave a different version of Burnett-Stuart's verdict – something like: 'Lt-Colonel Montgomery is a very good officer and is likely to reach the higher ranks of the army.'

Tim Pile† succeeded Gribbon. He just watched for six months. He was a gunner, and very good. Monty had written the new edition of the *Infantry Training Manual* in 1930. Though he had made some enemies, he had become wellknown in the Army. One of the other commanding

---

* General Sir John Burnett-Stuart (1875-1958) was GOC British Troops in Egypt 1931-34, and GOC-in-C. Southern command from 1934 until his retirement in 1938.

† Afterwards General Sir Frederick Pile (1884-1976), GOC-in-C, Anti-Aircraft Command, 1939-45. He commanded the Canal Brigade in Egypt, 1932-36.

The Mill stream at Isington

The view from the second floor window at the Mill

officers in the brigade in Egypt was Harold Franklyn,* who in 1940 commanded the 5th Division.

When Monty arrived back in Egypt in 1942 to command the Eighth Army he went to the Mena House Hotel for a wash and brush up. Auchinleck took him into his map room and shut the door. 'Only two people know what went on inside that room.' According to Monty, the Auk was obsessed with the idea that the Eighth Army was the only British army in the world and must be kept in being and not written off. If Rommel attacked again, as seemed likely, we might have to come back. Monty told me he said to the Auk: 'Well, I should have thought if that goes (pointing to the Alamein position on the map) you're done.'

'I knew Egypt well. I'd been stationed there for two years,' he said across the tea tray.

He felt that all the troops back in Cairo and the Canal Zone should be up in the Alamein Line. To this Auchinleck said 'no'. In the Monty version, he was difficult to talk to, was suspicious, and had a chip on his shoulder about the Indian Army. 'I said no more.'

I thought that the idea of moving 'all the troops' up to the front was ridiculous. If he meant infantry, artillery, maybe some tanks, that was one thing; but all the supply depots, the repair shops, the training schools and so much else were best left *in situ*. Moreover, Auchinleck was right to think of his troops as Britain's only army in the field, once we had lost 85,000 men in Singapore and had been forced to retreat from

---

* Lieutenant-Colonel, later General Sir Harold Franklyn (1885-1963) commanded the 1st Battalion of the West Yorkshire Regiment 1930-33, and was successively GSO1 and Commandant of the Sudan Defence Force 1933-38 before taking over command of the 5th Division.

Burma. Wellington had been cautious of *his* Peninsular army, because it, too, was the only army Britain could put in the field at the time.

Monty went on to say that he learnt on arrival in 1942 that officers from Eighth Army Headquarters had been off reconnoitring up the Nile Valley and choosing possible locations for Army HQ, half of them in Africa and half in Asia.

Apparently Bernard Freyberg*, an old friend, took Monty aside and said 'You've got to be a nice chap if you want to get on out here.'

Monty retorted that there would *have* to be changes and that in a few days he would *not* be a nice chap. General Ramsden†, for example, had, as Monty put it, been a very good commanding officer of the Hampshires in Palestine. But he'd gone on to become a corps commander. Monty left him in post till after the battle of Alam Halfa and then sent him away. In his opinion he was no good for a corps. 'He knew nothing about the conduct of war.'

This was one of Monty's sweeping, dismissive judgments which, as so often, overstated the case. However, he gave several more terse and largely favourable assessments of generals who had served under his command. Of Horrocks he said: 'As a CO, magnificent. But not a *grand chef*. He

---

* Lieutenant-General Sir Bernard (later Lord) Freyberg VC (1890-1963) commanded the New Zealand Division during the Second World War. He was Governor-General of New Zealand, 1946-52.
† Major-General W. H. Ramsden (1888-1969) assumed command of the 1st Battalion of the Hampshire Regiment in 1936 and served in Waziristan and Palestine. He commanded the 50th Division 1940-42 and, from July to September 1942 as an acting lieutenant-general, XXX Corps in North Africa.

rushed his fences.' Dempsey* Yes. Oliver Leese: 'You had to teach him, take him along with you.' He added that a *grand chef* cannot be foreseen until he commands a division in battle. He gave as an instance of this the fact that Alanbrooke spotted him commanding the 3rd Division before Dunkirk.

He admitted that he had once asked Nehru† about the business of a leader incurring odium and enmity. He stayed several times with Nehru and they ate their meals in the nursery, *en famille* (I noticed that Monty pronounced the double L, like 'meal',) – he and Mrs Gandhi and the children. One day Nehru and Monty took a walk in the garden and Nehru agreed that a leader must build himself up to his supporters. 'It's lonely at the top, and tough.'

He told me, for the second or third time, that Churchill had been very worried during the battle of Alamein. 'The rats at home were clamouring at him.' Had Eighth Army lost, Winston would have been out of office, so he always felt grateful for that victory in particular. Monty added cheerfully: 'I was always prepared to say: "Go to Hell!" '

He mentioned the Staff College and said they were trying to do the impossible in one year, and as a result turned out boffins. What was really important, in his view, was the handling of men – *command*. And the conduct of war. He himself had learnt most as an instructor at the Staff College and, later, chief instructor at Quetta**, as a full colonel.

* General Sir Miles Dempsey (1896-1969) commanded the Second Army 1944-45. Later he was C-in-C Allied Land Forces South East Asia and C-in-C Middle East.

† Jawaharlal Nehru (1889-1964), Prime Minister of India from 1947 until his death. Montgomery stayed with Nehru in New Delhi in January 1960. For further details see Chapter 6 of Montgomery's book *The Path to Leadership* (1961)

** He held the first post from 1926 to 1930 and was at Quetta for three years from 1934.

He told me that when he was a junior officer in India his weekly pay was £9, and the cheapest mess bill was £12, even if one was very abstemious.

At one point he referred to his Triumph car and his chauffeur, Michael Cox, who, I gathered, was allowed no cake or potatoes (presumably by Monty) because he was getting stout.

Monty told me he had given up foreign girls. Michael's mother, Mrs Cox, was the housekeeper, her other son Peter worked as gardener, and the unmarried girls also helped. His weekly staff bill was £50, he said. Two of the staff lived in the house whenever he was away, and one when he was at home. He went to bed at 8.30, having changed his way of life. For supper he sat on the sofa and had soup and toast on a tray. He enjoyed reading old favourites like *Robbery under Arms* by Rolf Boldrewood*, whom he had once met in Tasmania, and two books written by his grandfather, Dean Farrar: *Eric or Little by Little* and *St. Winifred's*†

He talked of the fantastic sales of *A History of Warfare* and of how much the four years' slog had taken out of him.

'I shall never write another book,' he said firmly.

Then he mentioned Slim's speech at the Foyle's Literary Lunch given at the Dorchester Hotel for the book, and quoted one sentence from it: 'Monty is always clear, even if you don't agree with him. I often don't!' Slim's reference to Montgomery as 'the most consistently successful general we have had since Wellington' gave him particular satisfaction.

---

* *Robbery under Arms* (1888) was written by Boldrewood, a pseudonym for T. A. Browne (1826-1915). He had been a squatter, a police magistrate and a commissioner of gold fields.

† *Eric or Little by Little* was published in 1858 and *St. Winifred's* in 1862.

Monty spoke of Oliver Leese and Slim, who was tired in 1945. Leese proposed that Slim should be sent to a base area or else sacked. According to Monty, Mountbatten agreed. When Alanbrooke heard of it he sent a signal 'What is this you have done? Such appointments are made by the Sovereign.'

Monty said he wouldn't go into the jungle with Mountbatten. As he did not watch television he had not seen John Terraine's serial programme entitled *The Life and Times of Mountbatten*.

'I know too much about Dickie,' remarked Monty with a glint in the eye.

The photograph on the mantelpiece of Mountbatten wearing naval uniform was inscribed:

To Monty	from	Dickie
M of A		M of B

He told me that in June 1947, when he stayed with Mountbatten while he was Viceroy of India, a particular mess waiter was appointed to serve Monty at dinner. Whereas all the other Viceregal servants wore a scarlet and gold uniform with buttons embroidered with the initials M of B, standing for Mountbatten of Burma, this particular waiter wore special buttons bearing the intitials M of A for the stay at the Viceroy's House of Montgomery of Alamein. I was amused by the story, but reflected on the trivialities of such great men.

Monty said that after the war Mountbatten used to ask him to suggest things to certain politicians – presumably ideas that Mountbatten wanted canvassing or supporting. Monty went on to say: 'Edwina had a heart of gold. She did too much, and it killed her.'* And then almost as if to redress the balance because he had spoken a bit unkindly of Mountbatten – I had noticed this trait in connection with other figures mentioned in the course of conversation – Monty added: 'Dickie and I are very good friends. I've often stayed at Broadlands.'† I sometimes wondered at the apparent paradox of Monty stopping with friends with whom he wouldn't go into the jungle.

Talk of Mountbatten led him to recall how on one occasion he had walked round the deck of the *Queen Mary* with Wavell.

'Did you know Wavell? One of my oldest friends.'

I had seen Wavell when he received an honorary doctorate at Cambridge University in 1946, and had once corresponded with him, but I had never met the Field-Marshal.

While walking round the deck, Monty had said to Wavell: 'You knew Neame** was no good. Why didn't you sack him? And why did you send O'Connor up to hold his hand?' (1941 in the Desert.)

A long pause followed this question. Then Wavell spoke. 'Perhaps I was wrong to do that.' He said no more.

---

* Edwina, Countess Mountbatten of Burma, died suddenly in North Borneo in 1960, while on tour as Superintendent-in-chief of the St John Ambulance Brigade.
† Mountbatten's house at Romsey, Hampshire.
** General Sir Philip Neame was in command of the reduced Desert Force under General Wavell in the spring of 1941 when Rommel arrived and began an offensive. Ordered to conserve forces and retreat, Neame was captured by the enemy together with General O'Connor, victor of Sidi Barrani, who had been sent to assist him.

XII

At the end of January 1969 I was stricken with a strange
illness which baffled the doctors at the Cambridge Military
Hospital as well as specialists at the School of Tropical
Medicine for many weeks while I underwent numerous tests.
In the end it was more or less agreed that I had an unusual
tropical bug, and this ebbed slowly away over the next six
years. Initially I spent five weeks in hospital and then paid
several short visits for more tests and more consultants, until
I felt like a prize exhibit.

I was thankful that my work on *A History of Warfare* was
already done before this absence from work. My return of a
book which the Field-Marshal had lent me several months
earlier prompted him to write:

If you had let me know I would have paid you a visit. I
know Webb, the medical specialist; he is good, and headed
a team which gave me a thorough check-up in July last
year. I have not been too well recently and finally had to
cancel all engagements, stay quietly in my home, and
recover my health. It is due to the unspeakable winter we
have had, and I had a series of colds and chills. Also I have
been doing too much for too long. I have now recovered,

but have to be careful not to overdo it. In fact, I am beginning to feel my age.

'Come over and see me some time.'

When I did so Monty spoke very warmly of Colonel Jack Webb* and the team of doctors who had examined him at Aldershot for four hours. Afterwards the doctors all went 'into a huddle'. Then Webb came and told Monty he must not do so much and must not rush about. Monty appreciated Webb's care, and on this we agreed wholeheartedly, because it was Colonel Webb who had looked after me so well and had been so persevering in his efforts to diagnose what was wrong.

Monty told me he planned to visit New Zealand next winter to stay with Sir Arthur Porritt,† the Governor-General. A year later he would go back to Cape Town and stay with a millionaire. He said his brother Donald in Vancouver was ill. 'He wants to see me again before he goes over Jordan.'** Monty mentioned his illness in Haifa before the war. He was getting no better and felt sure that if only he could go home to England, out of the sticky climate, he would improve at once. So he insisted, and he did get better at once – in time to take the 3rd Division to France in 1939.

Monty confided that he received a pension of £4,000 a

* Colonel J. Webb, MC, was Senior Consultant Physician at the Cambridge Military Hospital at the time.

† Sir Arthur Porritt was Governor-General 1967-72. He had served as a Brigadier RAMC under Monty's command in 21st Army Group. He was a very eminent surgeon, not least to the Royal Household. In earlier life he had been an Olympic athlete.

** Monty had to cancel one trip round the world in 1968 and another tour to Australia, New Zealand and Vancouver in 1969 on doctors' orders.

year as a field-marshal. The rank being still on the active list, this pension increased each time all service pay went up, whereas had he retired as a general, his pension would have remained stationary. He felt that Slim had been very poorly treated, as he had only an Indian field-marshal's pension. When he returned from serving as Governor-General of Australia he was very hard up. Even now, in his post as Constable of Windsor Castle, he would get a smallish salary and could never relax financially.

'Working for the Royal Family,' added Monty, 'is *not* well paid.'

Wednesday, 20th May 1970
In 1969 I had stayed at the Ecole Spéciale Militaire de Saint-Cyr at Coëtquidan, west of Rennes, and had lectured on the problems of jungle warfare to an audience of some four hundred student officers and staff. This had been a considerable ordeal and a test of my spoken French, but it had been well received. Now Lieutenant-Colonel Michel Camus, in charge of Military History at Coëtquidan, was paying a return visit – his second – to Sandhurst and was talking in French about his experiences while fighting in Indo-China prior to the French Army's defeat at the battle of Dien Bien Phu. Michel had commented wrily, when showing me to my room at Saint-Cyr; 'Is it mere coincidence that when French officers come to Sandhurst they stay in Waterloo Company Lines and that when you come here you have to sleep in Fontenoy* block?!'

It was my turn to look after him this Wednesday

---

* On 11th May French troops commanded by Marshal Saxe and watched by King Louis XV defeated an Anglo-British army at Fontenoy, near the Belgian town of Tournai.

afternoon. I drove him to Winchester to see the Cathedral, so tapestried with memorial plaques, many of them military, the College, and other good parts of that ancient city. I was wondering where to take Michel next when I had the sudden idea of calling on Monty on our way back to Camberley. I telephoned the Bentley number, explained about my visitor, and asked whether I might bring him in for just twenty minutes. To my relief, and slight surprise, Monty agreed at once, merely enquiring what time he was to expect us.

At Isington I led Michel Camus straight up to the Field-Marshal's sitting-room and introduced him. When I said that the Colonel had recently been conducting a special seminar on the Desert campaign of 1942 Monty seemed very pleased. He could not have been more friendly and asked me to pour out two glasses of sherry. Camus did not say much, since his English was hesitant and he was a little overawed at being in the presence of the famous Field-Marshal, but Monty soon put him at ease by talking about France and several French generals he had known such as Leclerc, Juin and de Lattre de Tassigny. He even launched into passable French from time to time, and Michel was quick to respond and appeared highly gratified at his reception.

Monty asked me in an undertone whether Camus read English fluently. I expressed doubts. Monty told me to go to the upstairs flat, where I had spent that arduous weekend under pressure working through the final typescript. 'On the table you'll find laid out various foreign editions of *A History of Warfare*. Bring me down the French one.'

I had seen none of these European editions, but soon identified the French version, Monty stood up, took out his pen, opened the volume on a table and then, having asked Michel Camus how he spelt his surname, wrote a personal inscription. This generous and kindly act gave immense pleasure. The Colonel fairly glowed, and the book became the envy of his colleagues at Coëtquidan as well as a treasured family possession.

The coloured dust-jacket, understandably different from that used on the British edition, which depicted the Battle of the Alma* in the Crimea reproduced another battle painting.

'Which battle is that?' asked Monty in his briskest style.

Beyond the fact that it was an eighteenth-century struggle, I did not know, and Michel was equally stumped.

Since the Field-Marshal seemed to be in no hurry to get rid of us, we spent three quarters of an hour at Isington before driving back to Sandhurst for dinner in the Mess. An unplanned and most rewarding sortie.

---

* On 20th September 1854 French and British troops under Saint-Arnaud and Raglan defeated the Russians at the Battle of the River Alma, the first Allied victory of the war.

XIII

Tuesday, 17th November 1970

I lunched at Farnham with Sir John and Lady Verney*, who showed me over the Maltings and the outside of several rather derelict adjacent houses which were to have been restored by the Farnham Trust. This was very kind of them, since they knew I was trying to buy a house in the town. After being introduced by Sir John to the managers of two bookshops and climbing up the Castle keep to look down over Farnham, I drove to Isington to have tea with Monty.

I always parked my car, pushed open the front door, walked up to the first floor and tapped on the half-open door of his sitting-room. Monty was seated on the sofa, reading. As so often, he wore a navy blue sweater and the blue and orange tie of the Royal Warwickshire Regiment. I gave him a copy of my new book *The British Soldier 1793-1815* and said he should regard it as a birthday present. I had just remembered that the 17th was his eighty-third birthday! He examined the book, asked a few questions about its publisher,

---

* Sir John Verney, MC, painter and illustrator, and author of the delightful *Going to the Wars*. His wife was fittingly called Lucinda. In 1970 he was Hon Sec of the Farnham Trust.

the date of publication, and the contents, then laid it beside him on the sofa, along with his reading glasses.

'I shall read it with great interest.'

He did seem to be genuinely pleased.

He asked me about the Sandhurst cadets, the shortage of numbers, the date and exact name of the new East Building. He had recently been to talk to the Staff College students. He spoke for ten minutes on the world situation as he saw it and then asked for questions. In response to one he had said that two things were vital to an officer. The first was a knowledge of the human factors – 'Our raw material is men.' The second was a knowledge of the conduct of war. Each was a lifetime's study. In fact, the business of war was just that. You had to give up a lot in order to study these two subjects. That was one reason why he had married late.

He told me his godson, Jeremy Soames, who had just left Eton, had decided he did not want to go into the Army. He had chosen journalism instead. 'You must *want* to be a soldier. When I joined it was because I wished to be a soldier.' He added: 'In those days we had a very amateurish sort of army.'

Reverting to the Staff College visit, Monty said he was too old for that sort of thing. He found it tiring. The talk had started at 11.30 and gone on with questions till 1.00. They should get someone younger. But the Commandant – 'Walker. What is his name?' 'Taylor,'* I said: this was the only time I saw Monty at a loss for a name or get one wrong – had said the young men wanted to hear him. But he could no longer do it so well. He had refused to lunch with the

* Lieutenant-General Sir Allan Taylor (1919-   ) was Commandant of the Staff College at Camberley 1969-1972.

students; just a private lunch with the Commandant.

After about twenty minutes Monty asked me to ring the bell to the left of the fireplace. Soon the housekeeper, dressed in brown, came in and placed a tray on the low table in front of the Field-Marshal. He poured out a cup of tea each. Then he cut me a large slice of home-made chocolate cake, but took none himself.

'I eat nothing – nothing at all after lunch except a glass of milk in the evening.' He found milk good for him, and took plenty in his tea. 'I must keep fit.'

He talked of men who could not stop working. 'I don't do anything!' I told him this might well be true on paper, but he was probably busier than many who did things, for he was much in demand and had so many visitors.

That was true, he said. Hardly a day passed without someone coming.

As often before he mentioned several of those who had died recently, such as General Sir Miles Dempsey. 'They're all dying, but I go on.' He said it with positive satisfaction.

This led him to talk of Basil Liddell Hart. Usually he and Kathleen had gone to Bournemouth in January to the same hotel as Monty – the Carlton. One day Monty had been to see him about his book, and thought he looked frightfully ill. He had been working far too hard on the proofs of the *History of the Second World War*, up half the night. When Monty left he said to Lady Liddell Hart: 'Will you see me out, Kathleen?' Then he told her Basil was obviously very ill and must see a specialist. It was arranged that he should see one after the weekend, but on the Thursday he had a heart attack, lay unconscious all day, and then died.

Monty had known him for fifty years, when Liddell Hart was Education Officer in Lichfield to a brigadier whose brigade-major, Tomes*, was an officer in Monty's regiment, the Royal Warwickshires. He had met Basil at Tomes' house.

Monty remarked that the reviews of Liddell Hart's last book had often been unfavourable. The balance of the book was wrong, and the chapters on Burma were hopeless. 'But there weren't any German generals there!' I said in defence that we all had our special interests and knowledge, though we must fall over backwards to avoid giving them undue prominence. Monty countered by saying that the fact that Liddell Hart had been a *military* historian, not a historian, showed in his book.

When Ludovic Kennedy had come to Isington to interview him about Liddell Hart for ITV – 'Do you know Kennedy?' – he had been asked how he would sum up the man. 'In one word, "kind". He was very kind to all who wrote or came for help, placing his archives at their disposal.' Kennedy had asked him why Liddell Hart's theories had not been accepted by the pre-war British generals, yet accepted by those in Germany. Was it pique? No. The generals did not consider the theories any good, but then the generals were awful. Only Jock Burnett-Stuart believed in them. However, maybe personal feelings had influenced some.

In fact, Monty once told Basil that if he had been CIGS in 1937 and Liddell Hart had been adviser to the Secretary of State for War, he, Monty, would have gone to the Prime

---

* Afterwards Brigadier C. T. Tomes, CBE, DSO, MC. He joined the Royal Warwickshire Regt in 1901, served on the North-West Frontier of India in 1908, and was twice wounded and decorated in France and Belgium during the 1914-1918 War. Tomes' final post before retiring in 1939 was Brigadier in charge of Administration, British Troops in Egypt.

Minister and said: 'As head of the Army *I* should be your military adviser. Am I this, or is it a retired captain?' Had the Prime Minister replied that it was the captain, Monty would have resigned. Basil had been angry to hear this; understandably so, I thought.

Later Monty mentioned the life of Gort that Jock Colville* was writing.

'Do you know him? Winston Churchill's private secretary.'

He told me you couldn't fault Gort as a man; absolute integrity, would never do anything mean or underhand. But as a soldier, not much good. He'd said so to Colville.

I asked Monty whether he had read Shinwell's† letter in the *Times* that morning about General Bob Mansergh;** who had died in hospital on the 8th aged seventy. Yes he had, but Shinwell had not told the truth. He had come to Monty one day and said: 'I can't get much out of this chap Mansergh (who was then Military Secretary). What's he like?' Monty had replied that he was excellent. 'Take him out to dinner, tell him stories, and make him tight. That should help.' Shinwell had done so, though whether he got Mansergh tight Monty never discovered.

* Sir John Colville was private secretary to Churchill for most of the Second World War and again from 1951 to 1955. His biography of Field-Marshal Viscount Gort was published in 1972 under the title *Man of Valour*.

† Emanuel, Lord Shinwell (1884-19   ) was Secretary of State for War and then Minister of Defence between 1947 and 1951. Montgomery served as CIGS 1946-48.

** General Sir Robert Mansergh (1900-1970) was appointed Military Secretary to the Secretary of State for War in 1948. He had been CRA and GOC of the 5th Indian Division, C-in-C UK Land Forces, C-in-C Allied Forces Northern Europe, and Master Gunner.

I expressed surprise that Shinwell should have used the word 'gloomy' of Mansergh, but Monty thought he was not very outgoing. Maybe he was shy, I said, but he was a very good speaker and a singularly charming man. Monty conceded that Mansergh was forthcoming once you got to know him. I told him I had come to know Bob Mansergh outside Baghdad in 1942, when he was CRA of the 5th Indian Division. Monty replied that Mansergh had served under Geoff Evans. This I knew, since Evans had commanded the Division for the late summer of 1944 until he was taken very seriously ill with scrub typhus.

Monty said that as CIGS he had sent Mansergh out to command British forces in Hong Kong, where he had Geoff Evans *under* him (commanding the 40th Division).

'Rather a case of box and cox for Geoff!'

I detected a note of malice in Monty's voice. I knew that he and Evans belonged to the Royal Warwickshire Regiment, and that relations between them had been strained. I disliked Monty for his petty attitude; still more for the fact that he had deprived Evans of the honour of becoming Colonel of his old regiment. I knew Evans's exceptional record as a brave fighting soldier in Eritrea, the Desert and Burma, with a triple DSO, as a commander whose sound judgement, brilliant decisions made coolly under intense pressure, and inspiring leadership were largely responsible for saving the Arakan front from collapse when the Japanese first attacked in February 1944. The part played a year before by Evans and his division during the battle of the Irrawaddy had also been outstanding. In any case, Evans and I had collaborated happily in 1958-62 over writing a book about the crucial battle of Imphal, and he was my friend.

I found Monty mean on this occasion. Perhaps it was as

well that I seldom knew the senior officers he talked of!

Aileen Cox came to collect the tea tray. We had each drunk three cups. Neither took sugar in tea. Monty said jokingly to the housekeeper: 'I can't make him have any more chocolate cake!'

'I've eaten two slices and it's delicious,' I told her, 'but I can't take any more.'

When she left the room Monty mentioned that he was going up to vote in a two-day motion of censure debate in the House of Lords. There were so many Labour peers that the Government might be in difficulty. He would lunch with Ted Heath. 'I don't think he's got a clue about what to do over inflation, and he ought to have. He talks of a long-term policy, but he ought to have a short-term one.'

Back on a military tack, Monty said that a commander must have time to think, whereupon I asked what power his chief of staff had had in Eighth Army. Monty explained that he had created a new system – was it so new? – by living forward in a tactical headquarters with a few officers and leaving de Guingand, who had considerable powers, to run the main HQ. If Monty was not available, de Guingand could take decisions, and every commander knew that an order from de Guingand was as if it had come from Montgomery himself. Freddie de Guingand was only a brigadier in 1942, but by virtue of his post as chief of staff he was senior to the other brigadiers at Army Headquarters such as Brian Robertson*. When the Eighth Army reached Tunis Monty had insisted that de Guingand be promoted to major-general.

* Brigadier Robertson (1896-1974), later General Lord Robertson of Oakridge, served as Quartermaster-General of the Eighth Army.

What, I asked, would have happened if Monty's caravan had been hit by a bomb and he had been knocked out? 'Very unfortunate', he replied. De Guingand, not the senior corps commander, would have carried on until someone else had been chosen to command the Army. This was a political appointment.

He added that it was probably a good idea to have a chief of staff at corps headquarters, but not at a divisional one, though in 1918 he had been virtually chief of staff when GSO1 in General Gorringe's* division.

I enquired when Monty had first met General de Gaulle. When he came to Normandy in 1944. He told me that while de Gaulle was out of office from 1946 onwards he used to visit Paris about once a month and take a room in a hotel† The General's presence was meant to be a secret, but Monty used to hear about these visits from his French ADC and then go and see de Gaulle.

Did they converse in French or English? Monty always spoke through an interpreter, but sometimes de Gaulle would tell the interpreter that he had followed what Monty had just said. He understood English fairly well. He hated the Americans and disliked the English, according to Monty. He had written to the General suggesting that he should stop at Colombey-les-Deux-Eglises, but he had not done so, because the French Government would not have liked it. However, he had several times driven through Colombey and waved, so to speak, to the de Gaulles.

---

* Lieutenant-General Sir George Gorringe (1868-1945) commanded the 47th London Division in France 1916-19 after war service in Mesopotamia.

† Hôtel Laperouse, 51 Quai des Grands Augustins, between the Pont Neuf and the Pont St Michel.

He got up from the sofa and showed me his inscribed copy of de Gaulle's latest volume of *Mémoires d'Espoir*, entitled *Le Renouveau*, and also the inscribed first volume of the General's *Discours et Messages*. He told me that de Gaulle had written in all his books and to prove the point he opened a glass-fronted bookcase on the left of the garden window and window seat – this was always piled with new books – and pulled out the English editions of the war memoirs. In each case the fly-leaf bore de Gaulle's handwriting in a personal inscription.

I commented, not without envy, that although he must have met almost all the famous people in the last thirty years, most of us had not done so, and as one of these I found that the two men I most envied others knowing were Churchill and de Gaulle.

Monty turned back to the bookcase and took out the other four volumes of the *Discours et Messages* and told me he didn't want them. Would the Sandhurst Library like to have them? I said they would be overjoyed. We shuffled the volumes, each bound in blue with a transparent dust cover, into the correct order. Only Volume One had been inscribed by the General. Monty said with a chuckle that had the other volumes also been inscribed he wouldn't have given them away!

XIV

Tuesday, 29th June 1971

I went to see Monty at tea-time, but he was not sitting on the sofa as so often in the past. Instead the housekeeper showed me to his bedroom which opened off the long sitting-room. Monty lay in bed, propped up by pillows and reasonably perky. It was reminiscent of my visit to him in King Edward VII Hospital at the end of 1963, except that on this occasion he was at home. A portrait of his father, the bishop, hung over the bed. Near the door was Eisenhower's indifferent painting of Monty wearing on his tunic the single ribbon of the American Legion of Merit.

Monty asked questions about Sandhurst, as he always did, because he took a genuine interest in what went on, in particular the quality of the officer cadets and changes in the methods of training. 1971 was for me the year of *War and Peace*. With two colleagues I was working as military adviser to the BBC for their Television version of Tolstoy's immense novel: first on uniforms, then on weapons and drill, next on orders and decorations, on military etiquette, on historical accuracy, and a host of period details. Monty wanted to hear about the work and about plans for going to Yugoslavia on location in August. But he tired more quickly than I had ever known him do, so after a cup of tea at the bedside I took my leave.

I was never to see him again. He was failing slowly, and received very few visitors: his family and one or two close friends. Now and then I would telephone and enquire from the housekeeper, Mrs Cox, how he was and whether he would like me to call in for twenty minutes. She went away to ask him, but invariably he preferred not, though appreciative of the thought.

However, I did have first-hand news of the old man from my Sandhurst colleague, Lieutenant-Colonel John Carver, one of Monty's two stepsons. He and his wife went to Isington from time to time, and at lunch in the mess at Sandhurst he would tell me about Monty. John and I had been sailing in Sandhurst's own yacht, the *Wishstream*, of which he was skipper for many years; and one weekend he had brought along Monty's son David for a cruise round the Isle of Wight.

No longer that clipped voice saying 'Bentley 3126' in reply to a telephone call; no more envelopes addressed in the familiar, clear yet faintly immature, laboured handwriting, with every *n* like an *m* and every *m* resembling a double *n*; no more letters beginning 'My dear Antony' and ending with 'Yrs ever, Montgomery of Alamein'; no more early Christmas cards; no more visits to Sandhurst. He lingered on for another four years. He passed his 88th birthday, and he died at home early on 24th March 1976.

I heard the news on the radio while driving to work from Petersfield. It came as a shock. I agreed with some of the instant tributes and took exception to other assessments which were hostile and denigratory.

Above all I felt saddened yet privileged. My life had been

enriched by our association, however tenuous. Better to have
helped him to make war and history from Alamein to
Lüneburg than to have helped him to write a history of war
from earliest times to the present day. Yet in itself that had
been an immensely worthwhile experience, and I shall always
be grateful.

Antony Brett-James – An Appreciation

Many readers will be saddened to learn that Antony Brett-James died, aged 63, on 25 March 1984, shortly after completing the present book. The news came as a tragic shock to his many friends and acquaintances, for although he had been dogged by severe ill-health from November 1980 (just seven months after his retirement from the headship of the Department of War Studies and International Affairs at the Royal Military Academy, Sandhurst), involving him in seventeen long months in hospital, everyone had hoped that he would have been able to continue his literary and scholarly contributions to the world of letters that meant so much to him throughout his life. But alas, this was not to be.

He was educated at Mill Hill School and at the Sorbonne. In the Second World War, as an officer in the Royal Signals attached to the 5th Indian Division, he served in North Africa and Burma (where he was Mentioned in Dispatches). After demobilisation he took his degree in Modern Languages at Sidney Sussex College, Cambridge, which had been interrupted by the war. He then entered publishing. It was at this time that his first book, *Report my Signals* (an account of his wartime experiences in the Far East), was published in 1948, followed three years later by *Ball of Fire*, a history of the 5th Indian Division; in 1953 there appeared *The Triple Stream*, a work on European literature from 1531 to 1930. By the mid-1950s he had also developed a strong interest in, and feeling for, the Napoleonic Wars, and in 1959 possibly his most important book, a biography, *General Graham, Lord Lynedoch*, was published; this was followed two years later by *Wellington at War (1794-1815)*, a selection of the Duke's wartime letters.

In 1961 Antony Brett-James left publishing to take up an appointment in the (then) Department of Military History at Sandhurst and he spent the remainder of his working life there, the last eleven years as head of the redesignated Department of War Studies and International Affairs. His established reputation as a military historian was further strengthened over the next two decades by eight more books. One, *Imphal* (written in association with Lt-General Sir Geoffrey Evans), published in 1962, was devoted to the great battle in Burma, 1944, in which both had served. The remaining seven were all connected with the Napoleonic era. He has bequeathed many of his papers to the Imperial War Museum, to form the Brett-James Collection for the benefit of future generations of researchers. Antony Brett-James was a frequent reviewer for *The Times Literary Supplement*, and contributed numerous articles to various magazines and part-works. In 1971 he was appointed senior military adviser for BBC TV's version of Tolstoy's *War and Peace*, and for the last ten years of his life he also regularly supplied questions for *Mastermind*.

One special task which brought him particular pleasure was his selection by Field-Marshal Montgomery to assist him in the preparation of *A History of Warfare*, and the fruits of this association between 1964 and 1968 form the basis for

Antony Brett-James – An Appreciation

Conversations with Montgomery, sadly his last book. It is evident that the two men struck up more than a purely working relationship over these four years; and just as many of the thoughts and comments of the great Duke of Wellington were noted down by such contemporaries as John Croker and Thomas Creevey, so Antony Brett-James may be seen to have carried out a similar role in his association with Monty during some of his later years for the benefit of posterity. His capacity for listening attentively was unrivalled.

Antony was essentially a shy, retiring, scholarly man, whose favourite pastime, as recorded in *Who's Who*, was 'browsing in antiquarian bookshops'. He also loved travel – until his illness made this impossible – and he enjoyed cultivating a wide circle of friends and acquaintances. At Sandhurst he always took a personal interest in the young officers and officer cadets he was asked to teach. Those closest to him knew Antony as a man of the greatest kindness, tact and integrity – always ready to help or advise a friend or colleague whether in the office, at his home in Petersfield, or, latterly, at Steep. He will be sorely missed by all who were privileged to know and work alongside him, and also by a wide and numerous range of readers who took the greatest pleasure, and gained much valuable knowledge and many insights, from his published works. These will long keep his memory green.

David Chandler
Department of War Studies and
International Affairs,
RMA Sandhurst.

June 1984

Index